PRAC
GOU
Company's
Coming®

Mostly
Muffins

Jean Paré

Front Cover

1. Cherry Flavour-Full Muffins, page 32
2. Sesame Cornbread Scones, page 115
3. Butterscotch Pumpkin Loaf, page 82
4. Cranberry Sparkle Muffins, page 11

Props courtesy of:
Linens 'N Things
Canhome Global

Back Cover

1. Cinnamon Swirls, page 111
2. Lemon Yogurt Muffins, page 22
3. Raspberry Muffins, page 28

Props courtesy of:
Cherison Enterprises Inc.

We gratefully acknowledge the following suppliers for their generous support of our Test and Photography Kitchens:

Broil King Barbecues
Corelle®
Hamilton Beach® Canada
Lagostina®
Proctor Silex® Canada
Tupperware®

Library and Archives Canada Cataloguing in Publication

Paré, Jean, 1927-, author
        Mostly muffins / Jean Paré.
(Original series)
Includes index.
Previously published: Edmonton : Company's Coming, 2006. ISBN 978-1-988133-32-4 (spiral bound)
        1. Muffins. 2. Bread. 3. Scones. 4. Cookbooks.
I. Title. II. Series: Paré, Jean, 1927- . Original series

TX770.M83P37 2017   641.81'57   C2016-905949-9

Distributed by
Canada Book Distributors - Booklogic
www.canadabookdistributors.com
www.companyscoming.com
Tel: 1-800-661-9017

We acknowledge the financial support of the Government of Canada.
Nous reconnaissons l'appui financier du gouvernement du Canada.

Funded by the Government of Canada
Financé par le gouvernement du Canada | Canada

PC: 38-4

Company's Coming Cookbooks

Quick & easy recipes; everyday ingredients!

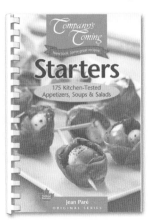

Original Series

- Softcover, 160 pages
- Lay-flat plastic comb binding
- Full-colour photos
- Nutrition information

Special Occasion Series

- Softcover, 176 pages
- Full-colour photos
- Nutrition information

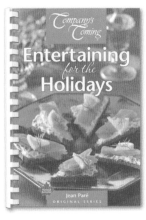

Original Series

- Softcover, 160 pages
- Lay-flat plastic comb binding
- Full-colour photos
- Nutrition information

Most Loved Recipe Collection

- Hardcover, 128 pages
- Durable sewn binding
- Full-colour photos
- Nutrition information

For a complete listing of our cookbooks, visit our website:
www.companyscoming.com

Table of Contents

Muffins

Loaves

Biscuits &
Scones

Specialty
Quick Breads

Allergy-Sensitive
Muffins

The Jean Paré Story

Jean Paré (pronounced "jeen PAIR-ee") grew up understanding that the combination of family, friends and home cooking is the best recipe for a good life. When Jean left home, she took with her a love of cooking, many family recipes and an intriguing desire to read cookbooks as if they were novels!

"Never share a recipe you wouldn't use yourself."

When her four children had all reached school age, Jean volunteered to cater the 50th anniversary celebration of the Vermilion School of Agriculture, now Lakeland College, in Alberta, Canada. Working from her home, Jean prepared a dinner for more than 1,000 people and from there launched a flourishing catering operation that continued for more than 18 years.

As requests for her recipes increased, Jean was often asked, "Why don't you write a cookbook?" The release of 150 Delicious Squares on April 14, 1981, marked the debut of what would soon turn into one of the world's most popular cookbook series.

Company's Coming cookbooks are distributed in Canada, the United States, Australia and other world markets. Bestsellers many times over in English, Company's Coming cookbooks have also been published in French and Spanish.

Familiar and trusted in home kitchens around the world, Company's Coming cookbooks are offered in a variety of formats. Highly regarded as kitchen workbooks, the softcover Original Series, with its lay-flat plastic comb binding, is still a favourite among home cooks.

Jean Paré's approach to cooking has always called for quick and easy recipes using everyday ingredients. That view served her well, and the tradition continues in the Practical Gourmet series.

Jean's Golden Rule of Cooking is: Never share a recipe you wouldn't use yourself. It's an approach that has worked—millions of times over!

Foreword

It's funny how a batch of blueberry muffins or banana bread can make the world a better place. Grumpy kids, just home from school, instantly brighten up when they catch the scent of fresh baking. Friends happily drop by for a cup of coffee and a heart-to-heart chat. Harried new mothers smile gratefully when presented with a basket of goodies. And tonight's surprise potluck invitation? No problem!

All this can be achieved with a few cups of flour and liquid, some flavourings and, most importantly, quick-rising ingredients such as baking powder or baking soda. In fact, it's the speed of the rising—much faster than yeast breads—that gives quick breads their name. Traditional loaves of rye or wheat take all morning to mix, rise and bake, but quick breads—muffins, loaves, scones, biscuits and specialty quick breads, such as coffee cakes—are ready in a fraction of the time. Parents of teenagers might add that the name has something to do with how quickly the results disappear!

Mostly Muffins will have your baking disappearing in record time. It follows the amazing popularity (over 1 million copies sold!) of our first quick bread cookbook, Muffins & More. In Mostly Muffins, you'll still find sweet offerings for breakfast and snacks, as well as savoury fare to accompany lunch or supper.

And with the growing interest in healthy eating, we've also incorporated wholesome ingredients such as flaxseed, wheat germ, whole wheat flour and nuts into many of our quick breads. Close to half of our recipes contain two grams of fibre or more per serving! As an extra benefit, we've clearly labelled recipes with three grams of fat or less per serving as low-fat. For those with allergies, we've included 11 special goodies, including Gluten-Free Honey Muffins and Eggless Pumpkin Muffins.

And since no baking cookbook would be complete without some decadent, special-occasion recipes, cast your eye over such treats as our Blueberry Cream Braid or our Roasted

Pepper Ring. Updates on old favourites, like Irish Soda Bread or Basic Carrot Muffins, are also in here.

Mostly Muffins will walk you through quick bread basics, starting on the next page. Then, at the beginning of each section, we've honed in on specifics for each type of baking.

So, pick a recipe and watch how fast your quick bread disappears!

Jean Paré

Nutrition Information Guidelines

Each recipe is analyzed using the most current version of the Canadian Nutrient File from Health Canada, which is based on the United States Department of Agriculture (USDA) Nutrient Database.

- If more than one ingredient is listed (such as "hard margarine or butter"), or if a range is given (1 – 2 tsp., 5 – 10 mL), only the first ingredient or first amount is analyzed.

- For meat, poultry and fish, the serving size per person is based on the recommended 4 oz. (113 g) uncooked weight (without bone), which is 2 – 3 oz. (57 – 85 g) cooked weight (without bone)—approximately the size of a deck of playing cards.

- Milk used is 1% M.F. (milk fat), unless otherwise stated.

- Cooking oil used is canola oil, unless otherwise stated.

- Ingredients indicating "sprinkle," "optional," or "for garnish" are not included in the nutrition information.

Margaret Ng, B.Sc. (Hon.), M.A.
Registered Dietitian

7

Tips for Terrific Quick Breads

Perfect whenever company's coming, a batch of freshly baked muffins or a warm golden loaf always look so cozy and inviting—it's hard to believe that it takes a whole lot of complex reactions to make them! But when you start mixing, for example, sodium bicarbonate (baking soda) with acids (buttermilk, lemon juice, etc.) and add heat, well, all kinds of interesting things can happen! Though quick breads are relatively easy to make, follow these suggestions for baking success.

- **Preheat the oven.** Quick breads need a hot oven to ensure even baking.

- **Use the correct pan size.** Use the pan size indicated in the recipe and fill each cup only as much as directed. Remember to leave room for the batter to rise if you are going to experiment with slightly different sizes. Generally, thinner cake-like batters rise more than thicker batters, so the thinner the batter, the more headroom you must leave.

- **Grease pans and tins, even if they're non-stick.** A coating of fat allows the sides of your baking to crisp—and it makes cleanup a snap. We use cooking spray in our test kitchen.

- **Use room-temperature eggs.** Leave eggs in their shell on the counter for 15 minutes, or place them in a bowl of room-temperature water for five minutes before using.

- **Cool melted butter before adding.** Hot liquids can cook any eggs in the batter earlier than required. Wait five minutes before adding melted butter.

- **Measure dry ingredients properly.** Ingredients such as flour, baking soda and baking powder need to be measured carefully. Use a dry measure (in which the contents reach right to the brim of the measure) for flour. Spoon flour into the measure, then level with the straight edge of a knife. Break up lumps of baking powder or baking soda with a fork before heaping into a measuring spoon, then level off. Too much baking soda can leave a soapy aftertaste while too much baking powder can leave an acid taste.

- **Mix the wet and dry ingredients in separate bowls.** Salt and leavening need to be distributed evenly throughout the flour before being combined with the wet mixture. Poorly mixed leavening agents can create a bitter taste.

- **A word (or three) about mixing:** *don't overdo it!* This can't be stressed enough. Stir until the flour is moist, but not smooth. Lumpy batter will produce light and tender quick breads. Keep your electric mixer in the cupboard.

- **Work quickly with baking soda batters.** Once you've combined the the wet and dry ingredients, spoon the batter into your pans and bake immediately. Refrigerator batters also contain baking powder, and may sit in the refrigerator before baking. Batters that have been stored in the refrigerator tend to be more dense than batters that are baked immediately.

- **Don't crowd your pans in the oven.** To ensure that your quick breads bake evenly, allow air to circulate around the pans. Two pans can be placed side by side, as long as there is at least a 1 inch (2.5 cm) gap between them, and between the pans and the oven walls. When baking three or four pans, stagger them on two racks so that no pan is directly under or over the other. Rotate them between the racks halfway through the baking time.

- **Always test for doneness.** Ovens vary, and baking times are guidelines. If a wooden toothpick inserted into the centre of your baking comes out clean, then it's done.

- **Don't remove items from pans and tins immediately.** Cool baking as instructed in each recipe. This will allow baking to release steam while holding its shape in the pans. But don't let it sit too long, or your quick breads will be soggy.

- **Refrigerate quick breads with perishable ingredients.** While most baking can be stored at room temperature for several days, items with meat, cheese or seafood need to be refrigerated.

- **Wrap lower-fat baking well.** Quick breads that replace some or all of the oil or melted butter with fruit purées are lower in fat and need to be well-wrapped or stored in an airtight container to prevent them from drying out.

Stock Up Your Freezer

Bake once and enjoy twice: our quick bread recipes are easily doubled. (We don't recommend tripling a recipe, however. It's better to make several batches.) Store any extra quick breads in the freezer for busy days or unexpected guests.

Place cooled muffins in a single layer in resealable bags and freeze, or wrap them individually first for grab-and-go snacks. Muffins thaw at room temperature in about two hours, four hours if they contain fruit. Loaf breads and specialty breads such as coffee cakes may be frozen for two months if they are wrapped in plastic wrap and aluminum foil. Let them thaw overnight before serving. You can also freeze individual slices of loaves and cakes for single servings.

Great Gifts

Fresh baking is always a welcome present, and quick breads are so easy to dress up. Here are a few ideas:

- Return an empty casserole dish or pie plate with a few loaf slices as a delicious thank you.

- Pop a dozen biscuits into an inexpensive, napkin-lined basket for your helpful neighbour.

- Wrap a coffee cake in foil, place in a large square of colourful tulle and gather with ribbon for a favourite teacher or coach.

- Bundle up a plate of bran muffins in a receiving blanket for a new mother.

Muffins

Well-made muffins are a handful of heaven. Moist, tender and bursting with flavour, they're always a welcome addition to any meal. Their small size appeals to kids and makes them a perfect choice for homemade fast food.

As with all quick breads, the key to magnificent muffins is to stir the batter just until it is moistened. Don't over-mix; small lumps in the batter are fine. For more general advice on baking muffins, please glance through Tips for Terrific Quick Breads on page 8. Below is some information specific to making muffins.

- Muffin tin sizes vary. In our test kitchens, we use 12-cup muffin tins with a scant 1/2 cup (125 mL) capacity in each cup. If your muffin cups have a smaller capacity, don't overfill them—this will cause the batter to run over the edges. Instead, add the batter to a new muffin tin, filling any empty cups with 1/4 inch (6 mm) water. This will prevent your tin from buckling in the heat. Be careful when removing the muffin tin from the oven as the water will be hot.

- Some tins make jumbo muffins or mini-muffins. Generally, a standard 12-cup recipe makes 6 jumbo muffins and, depending on the cup size, 36 mini-muffins. Bigger muffins will take longer to bake; smaller ones will take a shorter time. Check your baking frequently for doneness.

- Use a an ice cream scoop with a lever release to distribute batter evenly and neatly in the muffin tin.

Cranberry Sparkle Muffins

Use different colours of sparkling sanding sugar to correspond with a holiday or special occasion. Tart cranberries are a wonderful contrast to the sweetness.

All-purpose flour	2 cups	500 mL
Baking powder	1 tbsp.	15 mL
Salt	1/2 tsp.	2 mL
Butter (or hard margarine), softened	1/4 cup	60 mL
Granulated sugar	1/2 cup	125 mL
Large eggs	2	2
Vanilla (or plain) yogurt	1 cup	250 mL
Chopped fresh (or frozen) cranberries	1 cup	250 mL
TOPPING		
White sanding (decorating) sugar (see Note)	2 tbsp.	30 mL
Ground cinnamon	1/4 tsp.	1 mL

Measure first 3 ingredients into large bowl. Stir. Make a well in centre.

Cream butter and granulated sugar in medium bowl. Add eggs 1 at a time, beating well after each addition. Add yogurt. Stir. Add to well.

Add cranberries. Stir until just moistened. Fill 12 greased muffin cups 3/4 full.

Topping: Combine sanding sugar and cinnamon in small cup. Sprinkle on batter. Bake in 375°F (190°C) oven for 18 to 20 minutes until wooden pick inserted in centre of muffin comes out clean. Let stand in pan for 5 minutes before removing to wire rack to cool. Makes 12 muffins.

1 muffin: 196 Calories; 5.6 g Total Fat (1.6 g Mono, 0.4 g Poly, 3.1 g Sat); 48 mg Cholesterol; 33 g Carbohydrate; 1 g Fibre; 4 g Protein; 257 mg Sodium

Pictured on front cover.

Note: Sanding sugar is a coarse decorating sugar that comes in white and various colours and is available at specialty kitchen stores.

Orange Pumpkin Muffins

Fresh orange flavour in delicious harmony with pumpkin
and crunchy pecans. These are just perfect on a fall day!

All-purpose flour	1 3/4 cups	425 mL
Granulated sugar	1/2 cup	125 mL
Baking powder	1 tbsp.	15 mL
Baking soda	1 tsp.	5 mL
Ground cinnamon	1/2 tsp.	2 mL
Ground ginger	1/2 tsp.	2 mL
Salt	1/2 tsp.	2 mL
Large unpeeled orange, cut into eight wedges and seeded	1	1
Large egg	1	1
Canned pure pumpkin (no spices), (see Tip, page 83)	3/4 cup	175 mL
Pitted dates	1/4 cup	60 mL
Buttermilk (or soured milk, see Tip, page 13)	1/4 cup	60 mL
Butter (or hard margarine), melted	1/4 cup	60 mL
Chopped pecans	1/2 cup	125 mL
Pecan halves	12	12

Measure first 7 ingredients into large bowl. Stir. Make a well in centre.

Process orange wedges in blender or food processor until smooth. Add next 5 ingredients. Process until smooth. Add to well.

Add chopped pecans. Stir until just moistened. Fill 12 greased muffin cups 3/4 full.

Press pecan halves on top of batter. Bake in 375°F (190°C) oven for 18 to 20 minutes until wooden pick inserted in centre of muffin comes out clean. Let stand in pan for 5 minutes before removing to wire rack to cool. Makes 12 muffins.

1 muffin: 219 Calories; 9.6 g Total Fat (4.4 g Mono, 1.5 g Poly, 3.1 g Sat); 29 mg Cholesterol; 32 g Carbohydrate; 2 g Fibre; 4 g Protein; 353 mg Sodium

Pictured on page 107.

Apple Mince Muffins

Spicy and sweet—perfectly paired with a cup of coffee or tea.

All-purpose flour	2 cups	500 mL
Granulated sugar	1/3 cup	75 mL
Baking powder	1 tbsp.	15 mL
Salt	1/2 tsp.	2 mL
Ground cinnamon	1/4 tsp.	1 mL
Ground nutmeg	1/4 tsp.	1 mL
Large egg	1	1
Mincemeat	1 cup	250 mL
Unsweetened applesauce	1/2 cup	125 mL
Apple juice	1/2 cup	125 mL
Cooking oil	1/4 cup	60 mL

Measure first 6 ingredients into large bowl. Stir. Make a well in centre.

Combine remaining 5 ingredients in medium bowl. Add to well. Stir until just moistened. Fill 12 greased muffin cups 3/4 full. Bake in 375°F (190°C) oven for 20 to 22 minutes until wooden pick inserted in centre of muffin comes out clean. Let stand in pan for 5 minutes before removing to wire rack to cool. Makes 12 muffins.

1 muffin: 209 Calories; 6.0 g Total Fat (3.0 g Mono, 1.6 g Poly, 0.5 g Sat); 18 mg Cholesterol; 37 g Carbohydrate; 1 g Fibre; 3 g Protein; 245 mg Sodium

Pictured on page 107.

 tip To make soured milk, measure 1 tbsp. (15 mL) white vinegar or lemon juice into a 1 cup (250 mL) liquid measure. Add enough milk to make 1 cup (250 mL). Stir. Let stand for 1 minute.

Lemon Coconut Muffins

Zesty lemon glaze complements the toasted
coconut flavour. A tender and delicious muffin.

All-purpose flour	2 cups	500 mL
Medium unsweetened coconut	1 cup	250 mL
Baking powder	4 tsp.	20 mL
Butter (or hard margarine), softened	1/3 cup	75 mL
Granulated sugar	3/4 cup	175 mL
Large egg	1	1
Finely grated lemon zest	2 tbsp.	30 mL
Milk	1 cup	250 mL
Medium unsweetened coconut	3 tbsp.	50 mL
GLAZE		
Granulated sugar	1/2 cup	125 mL
Lemon juice	1/4 cup	60 mL
Water	3 tbsp.	50 mL
Finely grated lemon zest	1 tbsp.	15 mL

Measure first 3 ingredients into small bowl. Stir. Set aside.

Cream butter and sugar in large bowl. Add egg and lemon zest. Beat well.

Add flour mixture in 3 parts, alternating with milk in 2 parts, stirring after each addition until just combined. Fill 12 greased muffin cups 3/4 full.

Sprinkle with second amount of coconut. Bake in 375°F (190°C) oven for 18 to 20 minutes until wooden pick inserted in centre of muffin comes out clean.

Glaze: Combine all 4 ingredients in small saucepan. Heat on medium until boiling. Reduce heat to medium-low. Heat and stir for 2 minutes until starting to thicken. Carefully spoon over hot muffins. Let stand in pan for 5 minutes before removing to wire rack to cool. Makes 12 muffins.

1 muffin: 293 Calories; 12.3 g Total Fat (2.1 g Mono, 0.4 g Poly, 9.0 g Sat); 33 mg Cholesterol; 43 g Carbohydrate; 1 g Fibre; 4 g Protein; 199 mg Sodium

Pictured on page 71.

Basic Blueberry Muffins

Tender texture with plenty of blueberries. Just sweet enough. Try the lemon or oat bran variations below for a tasty surprise.

All-purpose flour	2 cups	500 mL
Granulated sugar	3/4 cup	175 mL
Baking powder	1 tbsp.	15 mL
Salt	1/2 tsp.	2 mL
Large eggs	2	2
Butter (or hard margarine), melted	1/4 cup	60 mL
Milk	1 cup	250 mL
Fresh (or frozen) blueberries	1 cup	250 mL

Measure first 4 ingredients into large bowl. Stir. Make a well in centre.

Combine next 3 ingredients in small bowl. Add to well.

Add blueberries. Stir gently until just moistened. Fill 12 greased muffin cups 3/4 full. Bake in 375°F (190°C) oven for 20 to 22 minutes until wooden pick inserted in centre of muffin comes out clean. Let stand in pan for 5 minutes before removing to wire rack to cool. Makes 12 muffins.

1 muffin: 197 Calories; 5.4 g Total Fat (1.6 g Mono, 0.4 g Poly, 3.0 g Sat); 48 mg Cholesterol; 33 g Carbohydrate; 1 g Fibre; 4 g Protein; 256 mg Sodium

Pictured on page 17.

LEMON BLUEBERRY MUFFINS: Add 1 tsp. (5 mL) grated lemon peel to egg mixture. Fill 12 greased muffin cups 1/2 full. Make small dent in batter with back of spoon. Spoon 2 tsp. (10 mL) lemon spread (available in the jam section of most grocery stores) into each dent. Spoon remaining batter over top. Bake as directed until firm to the touch.

Pictured on page 17.

OAT BRAN BLUEBERRY MUFFINS: Reduce all-purpose flour to 1 1/2 cups (375 mL). Add 1/2 cup (125 mL) natural oat bran. For topping, combine 1/4 cup (60 mL) natural oat bran, 2 tbsp. (30 mL) packed brown sugar and 1 tbsp. (15 mL) melted butter in small bowl. Sprinkle on batter before baking. Bake as directed for about 24 minutes.

Pictured on page 17.

Low-Fat Tropical Muffins

No added fat—and only the sugar from the coconut.
Tropical bits of pineapple, coconut and apricot in every bite.

All-purpose flour	3 cups	750 mL
Baking powder	1 tsp.	5 mL
Baking soda	1 tsp.	5 mL
Salt	1/2 tsp.	2 mL
Large egg	1	1
Milk	1/2 cup	125 mL
Vanilla extract	1/2 tsp.	2 mL
Can of crushed pineapple (with juice)	14 oz.	398 mL
Chopped dried apricot	1 cup	250 mL
Unsweetened applesauce	1/2 cup	125 mL
Medium sweetened coconut	1/2 cup	125 mL

Measure first 4 ingredients into large bowl. Stir. Make a well in centre.

Beat next 3 ingredients in medium bowl until frothy.

Add remaining 4 ingredients. Stir. Add to well. Stir until just moistened. Fill 12 greased muffin cups full. Bake in 375°F (190°C) oven for 18 to 20 minutes until wooden pick inserted in centre of muffin comes out clean. Let stand in pan for 5 minutes before removing to wire rack to cool. Makes 12 muffins.

1 muffin: 201 Calories; 2.0 g Total Fat (0.3 g Mono, 0.2 g Poly, 1.2 g Sat); 18 mg Cholesterol; 41 g Carbohydrate; 3 g Fibre; 5 g Protein; 258 mg Sodium

1. Lemon Blueberry Muffins, page 15
2. Oat Bran Blueberry Muffins, page 15
3. Basic Blueberry Muffins, page 15
4. Granola Banana Bread, page 93
5. Basic Banana Bread, page 93
6. Maple-Glazed Bran Muffins, page 43
7. Apricot Bran Muffins, page 42
8. Basic Bran Muffins, page 42
9. Chocolate Kissed Banana Bread, page 93

Props courtesy of: Cherison Enterprises Inc.
Danesco Inc.

Sunny Morning Muffins

Get your morning off to a sunny start with these lovely,
light-textured carrot and pineapple muffins.

All-purpose flour	2 cups	500 mL
Granulated sugar	2/3 cup	150 mL
Ground cinnamon	1 tsp.	5 mL
Baking soda	1 tsp.	5 mL
Salt	1/2 tsp.	2 mL
Large eggs	2	2
Can of crushed pineapple, drained	14 oz.	398 mL
Grated carrot	1 cup	250 mL
Cooking oil	1/2 cup	125 mL
Vanilla extract	1 tsp.	5 mL
Medium sweetened coconut	1/2 cup	125 mL

Measure first 5 ingredients into large bowl. Stir. Make a well in centre.

Combine next 5 ingredients in medium bowl. Add to well. Stir until just moistened. Fill 12 greased muffin cups 3/4 full.

Sprinkle with coconut. Bake in 375°F (190°C) oven for 18 to 20 minutes until wooden pick inserted in centre of muffin comes out clean. Let stand in pan for 5 minutes before removing to wire rack to cool. Makes 12 muffins.

1 muffin: 259 Calories; 11.8 g Total Fat (6.0 g Mono, 3.1 g Poly, 1.9 g Sat); 36 mg Cholesterol; 35 g Carbohydrate; 2 g Fibre; 4 g Protein; 232 mg Sodium

Pictured at left.

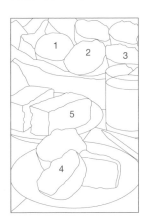

1. Sunny Morning Muffins, above
2. Big-Batch Apple Pie Muffins, page 47
3. Sunny Cranberry Muffins, page 41
4. Breakfast Muesli Muffins, page 138
5. Fruited Muffin Bars, page 132

Props courtesy of: Danesco Inc.
Mikasa Home Store

Spiced Fruit Muffins

All the true flavours of traditional hot cross buns in a fraction of the time.

All-purpose flour	2 cups	500 mL
Granulated sugar	1/3 cup	75 mL
Baking powder	1 tbsp.	15 mL
Ground cinnamon	1/2 tsp.	2 mL
Salt	1/2 tsp.	2 mL
Ground nutmeg	1/8 tsp.	0.5 mL
Ground allspice	1/8 tsp.	0.5 mL
Large egg	1	1
Milk	1 cup	250 mL
Cooking oil	1/3 cup	75 mL
Currants (or dark raisins)	1/2 cup	125 mL
Chopped mixed glazed fruit	1/2 cup	125 mL

Measure first 7 ingredients into large bowl. Stir. Make a well in centre.

Combine next 3 ingredients in medium bowl. Add to well.

Add currants and fruit. Stir until just moistened. Fill 12 greased muffin cups 3/4 full. Bake in 375°F (190°C) oven for 18 to 20 minutes until wooden pick inserted in centre of muffin comes out clean. Let stand in pan for 5 minutes before removing to wire rack to cool. Makes 12 muffins.

1 muffin: 221 Calories; 7.3 g Total Fat (4.0 g Mono, 2.1 g Poly, 0.8 g Sat); 19 mg Cholesterol; 36 g Carbohydrate; 1 g Fibre; 4 g Protein; 214 mg Sodium

Pictured on page 107.

HOT CROSS MUFFINS: Stir 2 tsp. (10 mL) milk and 1/8 tsp. (0.5 mL) vanilla extract into 1/2 cup (125 mL) icing (confectioner's) sugar in small bowl until smooth. Spoon into piping bag fitted with small tip or small resealable freezer bag with tiny piece snipped off corner. Pipe crosses onto cooled Spiced Fruit Muffins.

Banana PB Muffins

*Makes a flavourful substitute for the traditional
peanut butter and banana sandwich. Use either chunky or
smooth peanut butter. These will become a favourite!*

All-purpose flour	1 cup	250 mL
Whole wheat flour	1 cup	250 mL
Brown sugar, packed	1/3 cup	75 mL
Baking powder	1 tbsp.	15 mL
Salt	1/2 tsp.	2 mL
Large egg	1	1
Mashed overripe banana (about 2 small)	3/4 cup	175 mL
Peanut butter	2/3 cup	150 mL
Vanilla (or plain) soy milk	2/3 cup	150 mL
Cooking oil	2 tbsp.	30 mL
Mini semi-sweet chocolate chips	1/2 cup	125 mL

Measure first 5 ingredients into large bowl. Stir. Make a well in centre.

Beat next 5 ingredients with whisk in medium bowl. Add to well.

Add chocolate chips. Stir until just moistened. Fill 12 greased muffin cups
3/4 full. Bake in 375°F (190°C) oven for 18 to 20 minutes until wooden
pick inserted in centre of muffin comes out clean. Let stand in pan for
5 minutes before removing to wire rack to cool. Makes 12 muffins.

*1 muffin: 270 Calories; 13.2 g Total Fat (5.9 g Mono, 3.3 g Poly, 3.2 g Sat); 18 mg Cholesterol;
34 g Carbohydrate; 3 g Fibre; 8 g Protein; 276 mg Sodium*

Pictured on page 36.

Paré Pointer

Baby chicks like to play peck-a-boo.

Lemon Yogurt Muffins

Pudding powder makes for fast and convenient preparation.

All-purpose flour	2 cups	500 mL
Box of instant lemon pudding powder (4 serving size)	1	1
Baking powder	1 tbsp.	15 mL
Salt	1/2 tsp.	2 mL
Large eggs	2	2
Vanilla (or plain) yogurt	1 cup	250 mL
Milk	1/3 cup	75 mL
Cooking oil	1/4 cup	60 mL

Combine first 4 ingredients in large bowl. Make a well in centre.

Combine remaining 4 ingredients in medium bowl. Add to well. Stir until just moistened. Fill 12 greased muffin cups 3/4 full. Bake in 375°F (190°C) oven for 20 to 22 minutes until wooden pick inserted in centre of muffin comes out clean. Let stand in pan for 5 minutes before removing to wire rack to cool. Makes 12 muffins.

1 muffin: 192 Calories; 6.4 g Total Fat (3.4 g Mono, 1.7 g Poly, 1.0 g Sat); 37 mg Cholesterol; 29 g Carbohydrate; 1 g Fibre; 4 g Protein; 336 mg Sodium

Pictured on page 108 and on back cover.

Blueberry Cream Muffins

The rich flavour of sour cream also adds moistness to these biscuit-like muffins.

All-purpose flour	2 cups	500 mL
Granulated sugar	3/4 cup	175 mL
Baking powder	1 tbsp.	15 mL
Salt	1/2 tsp.	2 mL
Large egg	1	1
Sour cream	1 cup	250 mL
Butter (or hard margarine), melted	1/4 cup	60 mL
Fresh (or frozen) blueberries	1 cup	250 mL

(continued on next page)

Muffins

Measure first 4 ingredients into large bowl. Stir. Make a well in centre.

Combine next 3 ingredients in small bowl. Add to well.

Add blueberries. Stir until just moistened. Batter will be like biscuit dough. Fill 12 greased muffin cups 3/4 full. Bake in 375°F (190°C) oven for 20 to 22 minutes until wooden pick inserted in centre of muffin comes out clean. Let stand in pan for 5 minutes before removing to wire rack to cool. Makes 12 muffins.

1 muffin: 212 Calories; 7.6 g Total Fat (2.2 g Mono, 0.4 g Poly, 4.5 g Sat); 37 mg Cholesterol; 33 g Carbohydrate; 1 g Fibre; 4 g Protein; 248 mg Sodium

Mango Muffins

These tender, moist muffins have chunks of tangy mango in every bite.

All-purpose flour	2 cups	500 mL
Baking powder	2 tsp.	10 mL
Baking soda	1 tsp.	5 mL
Salt	1/2 tsp.	2 mL
Butter (or hard margarine), softened	1/4 cup	60 mL
Granulated sugar	1/2 cup	125 mL
Large eggs	2	2
Mango tangerine beverage	1 cup	250 mL
Chopped fresh (or frozen, thawed) mango	1 cup	250 mL

Measure first 4 ingredients into large bowl. Stir. Make a well in centre.

Cream butter and sugar in medium bowl. Add eggs 1 at a time, beating well after each addition. Add fruit beverage. Stir. Add to well.

Add mango. Stir until just moistened. Fill 12 greased muffin cups 3/4 full. Bake in 375°F (190°C) oven for 18 to 20 minutes until wooden pick inserted in centre of muffin comes out clean. Let stand in pan for 5 minutes before removing to wire rack to cool. Makes 12 muffins.

1 muffin: 184 Calories; 5.2 g Total Fat (1.5 g Mono, 0.4 g Poly, 2.9 g Sat); 47 mg Cholesterol; 31 g Carbohydrate; 1 g Fibre; 4 g Protein; 321 mg Sodium

Pictured on page 71.

VARIATION: Use orange juice instead of mango tangerine beverage.

Basic Banana Muffins

Dense-textured muffins. Banana chips add a special touch for brunch.

All-purpose flour	2 cups	500 mL
Brown sugar, packed	3/4 cup	175 mL
Baking powder	1 tsp.	5 mL
Baking soda	1/2 tsp.	2 mL
Salt	1/2 tsp.	2 mL
Large egg	1	1
Mashed overripe banana (about 3 medium)	1 1/2 cups	375 mL
Milk	1/2 cup	125 mL
Butter (or hard margarine), melted	1/3 cup	75 mL
Vanilla extract	1 tsp.	5 mL
Banana chips (optional)	12	12

Measure first 5 ingredients into large bowl. Stir. Make a well in centre.

Combine next 5 ingredients in medium bowl. Add to well. Stir until just moistened. Fill 12 greased muffin cups 3/4 full.

Press banana chips on top of batter. Bake in 375°F (190°C) oven for 20 to 22 minutes until wooden pick inserted in centre of muffin comes out clean. Let stand in pan for 5 minutes before removing to wire rack to cool. Makes 12 muffins.

1 muffin: 222 Calories; 6.3 g Total Fat (1.8 g Mono, 0.4 g Poly, 3.6 g Sat); 33 mg Cholesterol; 39 g Carbohydrate; 1 g Fibre; 4 g Protein; 255 mg Sodium

Pictured on page 71.

NUTTY BANANA MUFFINS: Use 1/2 cup (125 mL) smooth peanut butter instead of melted butter. Omit banana chips. For topping, combine 1/4 cup (60 mL) packed brown sugar, 1 tbsp. (15 mL) chopped salted peanuts and 1/4 tsp. (1 mL) ground cinnamon in small bowl. Sprinkle on batter before baking. Bake as directed.

BANANA WHEAT MUFFINS: Reduce all-purpose flour to 1 cup (250 mL). Add 1 cup (250 mL) whole wheat flour. Omit banana chips. Sprinkle 1/4 cup (60 mL) wheat germ on batter before baking. Bake as directed.

Muffins

Vanilla Pear Muffins

Take a break and enjoy these mellow pear muffins delicately scented with vanilla and cinnamon. The sprinkle of vanilla sugar forms a crispy crust on top.

All-purpose flour	2 cups	500 mL
Granulated sugar	1/2 cup	125 mL
Baking powder	1 tbsp.	15 mL
Ground cinnamon	1/2 tsp.	2 mL
Salt	1/2 tsp.	2 mL
Large eggs	2	2
Milk	1 cup	250 mL
Cooking oil	1/4 cup	60 mL
Vanilla extract	1 tbsp.	15 mL
Chopped drained canned pear halves	1 cup	250 mL
TOPPING		
Vanilla extract	1/2 tsp.	2 mL
Granulated sugar	1/4 cup	60 mL

Measure first 5 ingredients into large bowl. Stir. Make a well in centre.

Combine next 4 ingredients in medium bowl. Add to well.

Add pear. Stir until just moistened. Fill 12 greased muffin cups 3/4 full.

Topping: Combine vanilla and sugar in small bowl. Stir well until evenly distributed. Sprinkle on batter. Bake in 375°F (190°C) oven for 18 to 20 minutes until wooden pick inserted in centre of muffin comes out clean. Let stand in pan for 5 minutes before removing to wire rack to cool. Makes 12 muffins.

1 muffin: 206 Calories; 6.1 g Total Fat (3.3 g Mono, 1.7 g Poly, 0.8 g Sat); 37 mg Cholesterol; 33 g Carbohydrate; 1 g Fibre; 4 g Protein; 214 mg Sodium

Strawberry Rhubarb Muffins

Sweet cinnamon sugar atop not-too-sweet muffins. These freeze well—make sure to thaw the muffins uncovered to keep the sugary topping at its best.

All-purpose flour	2 cups	500 mL
Brown sugar, packed	1 cup	250 mL
Whole wheat flour	1/2 cup	125 mL
Baking soda	1 tsp.	5 mL
Salt	1/2 tsp.	2 mL
Large egg	1	1
Buttermilk (or soured milk, see Tip, page 13)	3/4 cup	175 mL
Cooking oil	1/4 cup	60 mL
Chopped fresh (or frozen, thawed) strawberries	1 cup	250 mL
Chopped fresh (or frozen, thawed) rhubarb	1 cup	250 mL
TOPPING		
Ground cinnamon	1/2 tsp.	2 mL
Brown sugar, packed	1/3 cup	75 mL

Measure first 5 ingredients into large bowl. Stir. Make a well in centre.

Combine next 3 ingredients in medium bowl. Add to well.

Add strawberries and rhubarb. Stir until just moistened. Fill 12 greased muffin cups 3/4 full.

Topping: Combine cinnamon and brown sugar in small cup. Sprinkle on batter. Bake in 375°F (190°C) oven for 18 to 20 minutes until wooden pick inserted in centre of muffin comes out clean. Let stand in pan for 5 minutes before removing to wire rack to cool. Makes 12 muffins.

1 muffin: 257 Calories; 5.8 g Total Fat (3.1 g Mono, 1.7 g Poly, 0.6 g Sat); 19 mg Cholesterol; 48 g Carbohydrate; 2 g Fibre; 4 g Protein; 240 mg Sodium

Pictured on page 53.

Mocha Hazelnut Muffins

A must-try muffin! Subtle allspice blends well with mild chocolate and coffee. Hazelnuts are the crowning glory.

All-purpose flour	2 cups	500 mL
Brown sugar, packed	1 cup	250 mL
Cocoa, sifted if lumpy	1 tbsp.	15 mL
Instant coffee granules, crushed to fine powder	1 tbsp.	15 mL
Baking powder	2 tsp.	10 mL
Baking soda	1/2 tsp.	2 mL
Ground allspice	1/2 tsp.	2 mL
Salt	1/2 tsp.	2 mL
Large eggs	2	2
Chocolate milk	1 cup	250 mL
Butter (or hard margarine), melted	1/4 cup	60 mL
Flaked hazelnuts (filberts)	1/2 cup	125 mL
Flaked hazelnuts (filberts)	2 tbsp.	30 mL

Measure first 8 ingredients into large bowl. Stir. Make a well in centre.

Combine next 3 ingredients in medium bowl. Add to well.

Add first amount of hazelnuts. Stir until just moistened. Fill 12 greased muffin cups 3/4 full.

Sprinkle with second amount of hazelnuts. Bake in 375°F (190°C) oven for 18 to 20 minutes until wooden pick inserted in centre of muffin comes out clean. Let stand in pan for 5 minutes before removing to wire rack to cool. Makes 12 muffins.

1 muffin: 260 Calories; 9.6 g Total Fat (4.8 g Mono, 0.8 g Poly, 3.4 g Sat); 48 mg Cholesterol; 40 g Carbohydrate; 1 g Fibre; 5 g Protein; 288 mg Sodium

Pictured on page 35.

Raspberry Muffins

A spicy streusel topping and a burst of raspberry make these special! Serve to your guests at the next coffee party.

All-purpose flour	2 1/2 cups	625 mL
Brown sugar, packed	1 cup	250 mL
Baking powder	1 tbsp.	15 mL
Salt	1/4 tsp.	1 mL
Large eggs	2	2
Sour cream	1/2 cup	125 mL
Butter (or hard margarine), melted	1/3 cup	75 mL
Milk	3/4 cup	175 mL
Fresh (or frozen whole) raspberries	1 cup	250 mL
Diced, peeled cooking apple (such as McIntosh)	3/4 cup	175 mL
TOPPING		
All-purpose flour	1/3 cup	75 mL
Brown sugar, packed	3 tbsp.	50 mL
Ground allspice	1/4 tsp.	1 mL
Cold butter (or hard margarine)	3 tbsp.	50 mL

Measure first 4 ingredients into large bowl. Stir. Make a well in centre.

Combine next 4 ingredients in medium bowl. Add to well.

Add raspberries and apple. Stir until just moistened. Fill 12 greased muffin cups full.

Topping: Combine flour, brown sugar and allspice in small bowl. Cut in butter until mixture resembles coarse crumbs. Sprinkle on batter. Bake in 375°F (190°C) oven for about 25 minutes until wooden pick inserted in centre of muffin comes out clean. Let stand in pan for 5 minutes before removing to wire rack to cool. Makes 12 muffins.

1 muffin: 318 Calories; 11.1 g Total Fat (3.2 g Mono, 0.7 g Poly, 6.5 g Sat); 63 mg Cholesterol; 50 g Carbohydrate; 2 g Fibre; 5 g Protein; 259 mg Sodium

Pictured on page 108 and on back cover.

Graham S'More Muffins

Everyone will be asking for s'more of these! Marshmallows and chocolate chips melted over graham cracker-flavoured muffins.

Graham cracker crumbs	1 1/2 cups	375 mL
All-purpose flour	1/2 cup	125 mL
Baking powder	4 tsp.	20 mL
Salt	1/2 tsp.	2 mL
Large eggs	2	2
Milk	1 cup	250 mL
Brown sugar, packed	1/3 cup	75 mL
Cooking oil	1/4 cup	60 mL
Chopped walnuts (or pecans), toasted (see Tip, page 95)	1/2 cup	125 mL
Miniature marshmallows	1/2 cup	125 mL
Mini semi-sweet chocolate chips	1/4 cup	60 mL
Mini semi-sweet chocolate chips	1/4 cup	60 mL
Miniature marshmallows	36	36

Measure first 4 ingredients into large bowl. Stir. Make a well in centre.

Combine next 4 ingredients in medium bowl. Add to well.

Add next 3 ingredients. Stir until just moistened. Fill 12 greased muffin cups 3/4 full.

Sprinkle with second amount of chocolate chips. Arrange 3 marshmallows on each muffin. Bake in 375°F (190°C) oven for 18 to 20 minutes until wooden pick inserted in centre of muffin comes out clean. Let stand in pan for 5 minutes before removing to wire rack to cool. Makes 12 muffins.

1 muffin: 230 Calories; 12.4 g Total Fat (5.2 g Mono, 3.9 g Poly, 2.5 g Sat); 37 mg Cholesterol; 27 g Carbohydrate; 1 g Fibre; 5 g Protein; 315 mg Sodium

Pictured on page 36.

Black And White Muffins

Dark cake-like muffins with a sweet cream cheese filling. Fancy enough for dessert and especially good served warm with ice cream.

Block of cream cheese, softened	4 oz.	125 g
Granulated sugar	3 tbsp.	50 mL
All-purpose flour	2 cups	500 mL
Granulated sugar	1/2 cup	125 mL
Cocoa, sifted if lumpy	1/4 cup	60 mL
Baking powder	2 tsp.	10 mL
Baking soda	1/2 tsp.	2 mL
Salt	1/2 tsp.	2 mL
Large egg	1	1
Milk	1 cup	250 mL
Butter (or hard margarine), melted	1/2 cup	125 mL

Beat cream cheese and first amount of sugar in small bowl until smooth. Set aside.

Measure next 6 ingredients into large bowl. Stir. Make a well in centre.

Combine remaining 3 ingredients in separate small bowl. Add to well. Stir until just moistened. Fill 12 greased muffin cups 1/2 full.

Make small dent in batter with back of spoon. Spoon about 2 1/2 tsp. (12 mL) cream cheese mixture into each dent. Spoon remaining batter over top. Bake in 375°F (190°C) oven for 18 to 20 minutes until firm to the touch. Let stand in pan for 5 minutes before removing to wire rack to cool. Makes 12 muffins.

1 muffin: 255 Calories; 12.9 g Total Fat (3.7 g Mono, 0.6 g Poly, 7.8 g Sat); 52 mg Cholesterol; 31 g Carbohydrate; 1 g Fibre; 5 g Protein; 344 mg Sodium

Pictured on page 35.

Rummy Eggnog Muffins

With eggnog flavours of nutmeg, cinnamon and rum, these muffins are filled with holiday cheer. Make these in a mini-muffin pan for afternoon tea.

All-purpose flour	2 cups	500 mL
Brown sugar, packed	2/3 cup	150 mL
Baking powder	1 tbsp.	15 mL
Salt	1/2 tsp.	2 mL
Ground nutmeg	1/2 tsp.	2 mL
Ground cinnamon	1/4 tsp.	1 mL
Large egg	1	1
Eggnog (see Note)	3/4 cup	175 mL
Dark (navy) rum	1/2 cup	125 mL
Butter (or hard margarine), melted	1/3 cup	75 mL
TOPPING		
Butter (or hard margarine), melted	1 tsp.	5 mL
Finely crushed gingersnaps	1/4 cup	60 mL

Measure first 6 ingredients into large bowl. Stir. Make a well in centre.

Combine next 4 ingredients in small bowl. Add to well. Stir until just moistened. Fill 12 greased muffin cups 3/4 full.

Topping: Stir butter into gingersnap crumbs in small bowl. Sprinkle on batter. Bake in 375°F (190°C) oven for 18 to 20 minutes until wooden pick inserted in centre comes out clean. Let stand in pan for 5 minutes before removing to wire rack to cool. Makes 12 muffins.

1 muffin: 242 Calories; 7.9 g Total Fat (2.3 g Mono, 0.5 g Poly, 4.5 g Sat); 43 mg Cholesterol; 34 g Carbohydrate; 1 g Fibre; 4 g Protein; 285 mg Sodium

Pictured on page 107.

Note: Use 3/4 cup (175 mL) buttermilk and 1/4 tsp. (1 mL) ground nutmeg when eggnog is not available.

Cherry Flavour-Full Muffins

*Pale pink muffins with cherry morsels and a burst of cherry jam
in the middle. Delicious with or without the jam centre.*

All-purpose flour	2 1/3 cups	575 mL
Baking powder	2 tsp.	10 mL
Baking soda	1/2 tsp.	2 mL
Salt	1/2 tsp.	2 mL
Butter (or hard margarine), softened	1/4 cup	60 mL
Brown sugar, packed	2/3 cup	150 mL
Large eggs	2	2
Cherry yogurt	1 1/4 cups	300 mL
Almond extract	1/2 tsp.	2 mL
Finely chopped maraschino cherries, blotted dry	1/2 cup	125 mL
Chopped walnuts	1/2 cup	125 mL
Cherry jam	1/2 cup	125 mL

Measure first 4 ingredients into large bowl. Stir. Make a well in centre.

Cream butter and brown sugar in medium bowl. Add eggs 1 at a time, beating well after each addition. Add yogurt and extract. Stir. Add to well.

Add cherries and walnuts. Stir until just moistened. Fill 12 greased muffin cups 1/2 full.

Make small dent in batter with back of spoon. Spoon 2 tsp. (10 mL) jam into each dent. Spoon remaining batter over top. Bake in 375°F (190°C) oven for 22 to 24 minutes until firm to the touch. Let stand in pan for 5 minutes before removing to wire rack to cool. Makes 12 muffins.

1 muffin: 299 Calories; 8.8 g Total Fat (2.4 g Mono, 2.5 g Poly, 3.3 g Sat); 49 mg Cholesterol; 50 g Carbohydrate; 1 g Fibre; 6 g Protein; 291 mg Sodium

Pictured on front cover.

FESTIVE CHERRY MUFFINS: Top batter with maraschino cherry halves before baking.

Chocolate Berry Muffins

*Sweet white chocolate is a delectable companion for
tart raspberries. Use paper liners for best results.*

All-purpose flour	2 cups	500 mL
Granulated sugar	1/2 cup	125 mL
Baking powder	1 tbsp.	15 mL
Salt	1/4 tsp.	1 mL
Large egg	1	1
Buttermilk (or soured milk, see Tip, page 13)	1 cup	250 mL
Cooking oil	1/4 cup	60 mL
Fresh (or frozen whole) raspberries	1 cup	250 mL
White chocolate chips	1 cup	250 mL

Measure first 4 ingredients into large bowl. Stir. Make a well in centre.

Combine next 3 ingredients in small bowl. Add to well.

Add raspberries and chocolate chips. Stir gently until just moistened. Fill
12 paper-lined muffin cups 3/4 full. Bake in 375°F (190°C) oven for about
24 minutes until wooden pick inserted in centre of muffin comes out clean.
Let stand in pan for 5 minutes before removing to wire rack to cool. Makes
12 muffins.

*1 muffin: 258 Calories; 10.3 g Total Fat (4.5 g Mono, 1.8 g Poly, 3.3 g Sat); 22 mg Cholesterol;
37 g Carbohydrate; 1 g Fibre; 5 g Protein; 184 mg Sodium*

Pictured on page 35.

Paré Pointer

*If you crossed an octopus and a mink, your fur coat
would have far too many sleeves.*

Lemon Cheesecake Muffins

Delicate lemon flavour with creamy cheesecake topping.

All-purpose flour	2 cups	500 mL
Granulated sugar	1/2 cup	125 mL
Baking powder	1 tbsp.	15 mL
Salt	1/2 tsp.	2 mL
Cold butter (or hard margarine), cut up	1/3 cup	75 mL
Large egg	1	1
Milk	1/2 cup	125 mL
Sour cream	1/2 cup	125 mL
Lemon juice	2 tbsp.	30 mL
Grated lemon zest	1 tbsp.	15 mL
Block of cream cheese, softened	4 oz.	125 g
Sour cream	1/4 cup	60 mL
Granulated sugar	4 tsp.	20 mL

Measure first 4 ingredients into large bowl. Stir. Cut in butter until mixture resembles coarse crumbs. Make a well in centre.

Combine next 5 ingredients in small bowl. Add to well. Stir until just moistened. Fill 12 greased muffin cups 3/4 full.

Mash remaining 3 ingredients in small bowl. Spread on batter. Bake in 375°F (190°C) oven for 20 to 22 minutes until wooden pick inserted in centre of muffin comes out clean and tops start to brown. Let stand in pan for 5 minutes before removing to wire rack to cool. Makes 12 muffins.

1 muffin: 239 Calories; 11.9 g Total Fat (3.4 g Mono, 0.6 g Poly, 7.2 g Sat); 50 mg Cholesterol; 29 g Carbohydrate; 1 g Fibre; 4 g Protein; 295 mg Sodium

Props courtesy of: Cherison Enterprises Inc.

Muffins

Jambuster Muffins

These firm oatmeal muffins explode with raspberry flavour in every bite. Try these with your favourite flavour of jam.

All-purpose flour	2 cups	500 mL
Quick-cooking rolled oats	1 cup	250 mL
Brown sugar, packed	1/2 cup	125 mL
Baking powder	1 tbsp.	15 mL
Ground cinnamon	1/2 tsp.	2 mL
Salt	1/2 tsp.	2 mL
Large eggs	2	2
Milk	1 cup	250 mL
Cooking oil	1/4 cup	60 mL
Seedless raspberry jam (not jelly)	1/2 cup	125 mL

Measure first 6 ingredients into large bowl. Stir. Make a well in centre.

Combine next 3 ingredients in medium bowl. Add to well. Stir until just moistened. Fill 12 greased muffin cups 1/2 full.

Make small dent in batter with back of spoon. Spoon 2 tsp. (10 mL) jam into each dent. Spoon remaining batter over top. Bake in 375°F (190°C) oven for 18 to 20 minutes until firm to the touch. Let stand in pan for 5 minutes before removing to wire rack to cool. Makes 12 muffins.

1 muffin: 249 Calories; 6.7 g Total Fat (3.5 g Mono, 1.9 g Poly, 0.9 g Sat); 37 mg Cholesterol; 43 g Carbohydrate; 2 g Fibre; 5 g Protein; 223 mg Sodium

1. Banana PB Muffins, page 21
2. Pizza Muffins, page 69
3. Masa Taco Muffins, page 76
4. Graham S'More Muffins, page 29

Apricot Flavour-Full Muffins

Moist, golden muffins oozing with sweet apricot
filling. Crunchy walnuts throughout.

Boiling water	1 cup	250 mL
Finely chopped dried apricot	3/4 cup	175 mL
All-purpose flour	2 cups	500 mL
Chopped walnuts (or pecans)	1/2 cup	125 mL
Baking powder	1 tbsp.	15 mL
Salt	1/2 tsp.	2 mL
Baking soda	1/4 tsp.	1 mL
Butter (or hard margarine), softened	1/4 cup	60 mL
Granulated sugar	2/3 cup	150 mL
Large egg	1	1
Apricot nectar	1/2 cup	125 mL
Milk	1/4 cup	60 mL
Lemon juice	1 tsp.	5 mL
Apricot jam	1/2 cup	125 mL

Pour boiling water over apricot in small heatproof bowl. Let stand for 10 minutes until softened. Drain well. Set aside.

Measure next 5 ingredients into large bowl. Stir. Make a well in centre.

Cream butter and sugar in medium bowl. Add egg. Beat well. Add next 3 ingredients. Stir. Add to well. Add apricot. Stir until just moistened. Fill 12 greased muffin cups 1/2 full.

Make small dent in batter with back of spoon. Spoon 2 tsp. (10 mL) jam into dents. Spoon remaining batter over top. Bake in 375°F (190°C) oven for 18 to 20 minutes until firm to the touch. Let stand in pan for 5 minutes before removing to wire rack to cool. Makes 12 muffins.

1 muffin: 265 Calories; 8.0 g Total Fat (2.1 g Mono, 2.4 g Poly, 2.9 g Sat); 29 mg Cholesterol; 46 g Carbohydrate; 2 g Fibre; 5 g Protein; 275 mg Sodium

VARIATION: Use peach, mango or raspberry jam, or ginger marmalade instead of apricot jam.

Muffins

Fig Centre Muffins

Orange wheat muffins with sweet and crunchy fig filling. Flavour is reminiscent of the famous Fig Newton cookie. Attractive nut topping.

Dried figs, chopped	1/2 cup	125 mL
Orange juice	3 tbsp.	50 mL
Flaked hazelnuts (filberts), toasted (see Tip, page 95)	2 tbsp.	30 mL
Liquid honey	1 tbsp.	15 mL
Ground cinnamon	1/4 tsp.	1 mL
All-purpose flour	1 1/4 cups	300 mL
Whole wheat flour	1 cup	250 mL
Wheat germ, toasted (see Tip, page 45)	1/4 cup	60 mL
Baking powder	2 tsp.	10 mL
Baking soda	1/2 tsp.	2 mL
Salt	1/2 tsp.	2 mL
Large eggs	2	2
Vanilla yogurt	1 cup	250 mL
Brown sugar, packed	1/2 cup	125 mL
Orange juice	1/2 cup	125 mL
Cooking oil	1/4 cup	60 mL
Grated orange zest	2 tsp.	10 mL
Chopped flaked hazelnuts (filberts)	1/4 cup	60 mL

Process first 5 ingredients in blender or food processor until almost smooth. Set aside.

Measure next 6 ingredients into large bowl. Stir. Make a well in centre.

Combine next 6 ingredients in small bowl. Add to well. Stir until just moistened. Fill 12 greased muffin cups 1/2 full. Make small dent in batter with back of spoon. Spoon about 2 tsp. (10 mL) fig mixture into each dent. Spoon remaining batter over top.

Sprinkle with second amount of hazelnuts. Bake in 375°F (190°C) oven for 18 to 20 minutes until firm to the touch. Let stand in pan for 5 minutes before removing to wire rack to cool. Makes 12 muffins.

1 muffin: 267 Calories; 9.2 g Total Fat (5.2 g Mono, 2.1 g Poly, 1.2 g Sat); 37 mg Cholesterol; 42 g Carbohydrate; 3 g Fibre; 6 g Protein; 243 mg Sodium

Basic Oatmeal Muffins

Try the tasty variations of this wholesome favorite.

Quick-cooking rolled oats	1 1/2 cups	375 mL
Buttermilk (or soured milk, see Tip, page 13)	1 1/2 cups	375 mL
All-purpose flour	1 1/2 cups	375 mL
Brown sugar, packed	3/4 cup	175 mL
Ground cinnamon	1 1/2 tsp.	7 mL
Baking powder	1 1/2 tsp.	7 mL
Baking soda	3/4 tsp.	4 mL
Salt	3/4 tsp.	4 mL
Large eggs, fork-beaten	2	2
Butter (or hard margarine), melted	1/3 cup	75 mL
TOPPING		
Quick-cooking rolled oats	1/4 cup	60 mL
Brown sugar, packed	2 tbsp.	30 mL
Ground cinnamon	1/4 tsp.	1 mL

Combine first amount of rolled oats and buttermilk in small bowl. Let stand for 10 minutes.

Measure next 6 ingredients into large bowl. Make a well in centre.

Stir eggs and butter into oatmeal mixture. Add to well. Stir until just moistened. Fill 12 greased muffin cups full.

Topping: Combine all 3 ingredients in small bowl. Sprinkle on batter. Bake in 375°F (190°C) oven for 18 to 20 minutes until wooden pick inserted in centre of muffin comes out clean. Let stand in pan for 5 minutes before removing to wire rack to cool. Makes 12 muffins.

1 muffin: 257 Calories; 7.7 g Total Fat (2.3 g Mono, 0.8 g Poly, 4.0 g Sat); 52 mg Cholesterol; 41 g Carbohydrate; 2 g Fibre; 6 g Protein; 382 mg Sodium

SPICY OATMEAL MUFFINS: Use the same amount of Chinese five-spice powder instead of cinnamon in both batter and topping. Bake as directed.

APPLE OATMEAL MUFFINS: Add 1 2/3 cups (400 mL) grated peeled cooking apple (such as McIntosh) to egg mixture. Decrease butter (or hard margarine) to 2 tbsp. (30 mL). Bake as directed.

Muffins

Sunny Cranberry Muffins

Loaded with chewy cranberries and topped with toasted
sunflower seeds. Enjoy the orange fragrance while they bake.

All-purpose flour	1 cup	250 mL
Whole wheat flour	1 cup	250 mL
Brown sugar, packed	1/2 cup	125 mL
Baking powder	1 tbsp.	15 mL
Salt	1/4 tsp.	1 mL
Large egg	1	1
Can of evaporated milk	5 1/2 oz.	160 mL
Orange juice	1/3 cup	75 mL
Cooking oil	1/4 cup	60 mL
Grated orange zest	2 tsp.	10 mL
Dried cranberries	1 cup	250 mL
Unsalted, roasted sunflower seeds	1/4 cup	60 mL

Measure first 5 ingredients into large bowl. Stir. Make a well in centre.

Beat next 5 ingredients in medium bowl. Add to well.

Add cranberries. Stir until just moistened. Fill 12 greased muffin cups 3/4 full.

Sprinkle with sunflower seeds. Bake in 375°F (190°C) oven for 20 to 22 minutes until wooden pick inserted in centre of muffin comes out clean. Let stand in pan for 5 minutes before removing to wire rack to cool. Makes 12 muffins.

1 muffin: 218 Calories; 8.2 g Total Fat (3.7 g Mono, 2.6 g Poly, 1.4 g Sat); 22 mg Cholesterol; 33 g Carbohydrate; 3 g Fibre; 5 g Protein; 167 mg Sodium

Pictured on page 18.

Paré Pointer
A pig writes letters with a pig pen.

Basic Bran Muffins

A classic bran and molasses muffin. The variations
below have added goodness for special company.

Buttermilk (or soured milk, see Tip, page 13)	1 cup	250 mL
Natural wheat bran	1 cup	250 mL
All-purpose flour	1 1/4 cups	300 mL
Brown sugar, packed	1/4 cup	60 mL
Baking powder	1 tsp.	5 mL
Baking soda	1 tsp.	5 mL
Salt	1/2 tsp.	2 mL
Large egg, fork-beaten	1	1
Fancy (mild) molasses	1/4 cup	60 mL
Cooking oil	1/4 cup	60 mL
Vanilla extract	1 tsp.	5 mL

Stir buttermilk into bran in medium bowl. Let stand for 10 minutes.

Measure next 5 ingredients into large bowl. Stir. Make a well in centre.

Stir remaining 4 ingredients into bran mixture. Add to well. Stir until just moistened. Fill 12 greased muffin cups 3/4 full. Bake in 375°F (190°C) oven for 20 to 22 minutes until wooden pick inserted in centre of muffin comes out clean. Let stand in pan for 5 minutes before removing to wire rack to cool. Makes 12 muffins.

1 muffin: 158 Calories; 5.8 g Total Fat (3.1 g Mono, 1.7 g Poly, 0.7 g Sat); 19 mg Cholesterol; 25 g Carbohydrate; 3 g Fibre; 3 g Protein; 270 mg Sodium

Pictured on page 17.

APRICOT BRAN MUFFINS: Add 1/2 cup (125 mL) chopped dried apricot (or other dried fruit) and 1/2 cup (125 mL) chopped almonds (or walnuts, pecans or hazelnuts) when adding bran mixture to flour mixture. Bake as directed.

Pictured on page 17.

ZUCCHINI BRAN MUFFINS: Stir 1 cup (250 mL) grated unpeeled zucchini into bran mixture before adding to flour mixture. Bake as directed.

(continued on next page)

MAPLE-GLAZED BRAN MUFFINS: Use 1/4 cup (60 mL) maple (or maple-flavoured) syrup instead of molasses. Bake as directed. Combine 1 tbsp. (15 mL) softened butter (or hard margarine), 1/4 cup (60 mL) icing (confectioner's) sugar and 1 1/2 tbsp. (25 mL) maple (or maple-flavoured) syrup in small bowl. Drizzle over warm baked muffins.

Pictured on page 17.

Nutty Cream Carrot Muffins

The delicious, creamy walnut topping makes these
extra special. Lots of carrot and a hint of orange flavour.

Block of cream cheese, softened	4 oz.	125 g
Sour cream	1/4 cup	60 mL
Granulated sugar	4 tsp.	20 mL
Finely chopped walnuts	1/4 cup	60 mL
All-purpose flour	1 3/4 cups	425 mL
Whole wheat flour	1/2 cup	125 mL
Brown sugar, packed	1/2 cup	125 mL
Baking soda	2 tsp.	10 mL
Salt	1/2 tsp.	2 mL
Large eggs	2	2
Grated carrot	1 1/2 cups	375 mL
Buttermilk (or soured milk, see Tip, page 13)	1 cup	250 mL
Frozen concentrated orange juice, thawed	3 tbsp.	50 mL
Cooking oil	3 tbsp.	50 mL
Vanilla extract	1 tsp.	5 mL

Combine first 3 ingredients in small bowl. Add walnuts. Stir. Set aside.

Measure next 5 ingredients into large bowl. Stir. Make a well in centre.

Combine remaining 6 ingredients in medium bowl. Add to well. Stir until just moistened. Fill 12 greased muffin cups full. Spread cream cheese mixture on batter. Bake in 375°F (190°C) oven for 18 to 20 minutes until wooden pick inserted in centre of muffin comes out clean. Let stand in pan for 5 minutes before removing to wire rack to cool. Makes 12 muffins.

1 muffin: 256 Calories; 10.7 g Total Fat (4.0 g Mono, 2.5 g Poly, 3.5 g Sat); 50 mg Cholesterol; 35 g Carbohydrate; 2 g Fibre; 6 g Protein; 388 mg Sodium

Pictured on page 54.

Nutty Flax Muffins

*Naturally sweet dates and toasted walnuts unite in these delicious muffins.
Large and hearty—try one for a healthy breakfast or snack.*

Whole wheat flour	1 cup	250 mL
All-purpose flour	1 cup	250 mL
Ground flaxseed (see Tip, page 51)	1/4 cup	60 mL
Ground cinnamon	1 1/2 tsp.	7 mL
Baking powder	1 1/2 tsp.	7 mL
Baking soda	1/2 tsp.	2 mL
Salt	1/4 tsp.	1 mL
Large eggs, fork-beaten	2	2
Buttermilk (or soured milk, see Tip, page 13)	1 cup	250 mL
Maple (or maple-flavoured) syrup	1/2 cup	125 mL
Cooking oil	1/4 cup	60 mL
Frozen concentrated orange juice, thawed	2 tbsp.	30 mL
Vanilla extract	1 tsp.	5 mL
Chopped pitted dates	1 1/4 cups	300 mL
Chopped walnuts, toasted (see Tip, page 95)	3/4 cup	175 mL

Measure first 7 ingredients into large bowl. Stir. Make a well in centre.

Combine next 6 ingredients in medium bowl. Add to well.

Add dates and walnuts. Stir until just moistened. Fill 12 greased muffin
cups full. Bake in 375°F (190°C) oven for 18 to 20 minutes until wooden
pick inserted in centre of muffin comes out clean. Let stand in pan for
5 minutes before removing to wire rack to cool. Makes 12 muffins.

*1 muffin: 304 Calories; 12.1 g Total Fat (4.5 g Mono, 5.5 g Poly, 1.2 g Sat); 37 mg Cholesterol;
45 g Carbohydrate; 4 g Fibre; 7 g Protein; 187 mg Sodium*

Fig Bran Muffins

The perfect breakfast muffins to start your morning off right!

Large eggs	2	2
Buttermilk (or soured milk, see Tip, page 13)	1 1/2 cups	375 mL
Unsweetened applesauce	1/4 cup	60 mL
Cooking oil	1/4 cup	60 mL
Vanilla extract	1 1/2 tsp.	7 mL
All-bran cereal	1 1/2 cups	375 mL
Whole wheat flour	1 3/4 cups	425 mL
Brown sugar, packed	3/4 cup	175 mL
Baking soda	1 1/2 tsp.	7 mL
Ground allspice	1/2 tsp.	2 mL
Salt	1/2 tsp.	2 mL
Chopped dried figs	1 1/2 cups	375 mL

Combine first 5 ingredients in medium bowl. Add cereal. Stir. Let stand for 10 minutes.

Measure next 5 ingredients into large bowl. Stir. Make a well in centre.

Add figs and cereal mixture to well. Stir until just moistened. Fill 12 greased muffin cups full. Bake in 375°F (190°C) oven for 18 to 20 minutes until wooden pick inserted in centre of muffin comes out clean. Let stand in pan for 5 minutes before removing to wire rack to cool. Makes 12 muffins.

1 muffin: 272 Calories; 6.8 g Total Fat (3.4 g Mono, 1.8 g Poly, 0.9 g Sat); 37 mg Cholesterol; 52 g Carbohydrate; 8 g Fibre; 6 g Protein; 393 mg Sodium

 tip To toast wheat germ, spread evenly in an ungreased shallow frying pan. Heat and stir on medium until golden. To bake, spread evenly in an ungreased shallow pan. Bake in a 350°F (175°C) oven for 3 minutes, stirring or shaking often, until golden. Cool before adding to recipe.

Basic Carrot Muffins

Moist muffins with hints of cinnamon and nutmeg. The variations below are also delicious and uniquely different in flavour.

All-purpose flour	2 cups	500 mL
Brown sugar, packed	2/3 cup	150 mL
Baking powder	1 tsp.	5 mL
Baking soda	1/2 tsp.	2 mL
Salt	1/2 tsp.	2 mL
Ground cinnamon	1/2 tsp.	2 mL
Ground nutmeg	1/4 tsp.	1 mL
Large eggs, fork-beaten	2	2
Buttermilk (or soured milk, see Tip, page 13)	3/4 cup	175 mL
Cooking oil	1/3 cup	75 mL
Vanilla extract	1/2 tsp.	2 mL
Grated carrot	1 1/2 cups	375 mL

Measure first 7 ingredients into large bowl. Stir. Make a well in centre.

Combine next 4 ingredients in medium bowl. Add to well.

Add carrot. Stir until just moistened. Fill 12 greased muffin cups 3/4 full. Bake in 375°F (190°C) oven for 20 to 22 minutes until wooden pick inserted in centre of muffin comes out clean. Let stand in pan for 5 minutes before removing to wire rack to cool. Makes 12 muffins.

1 muffin: 212 Calories; 7.6 g Total Fat (4.1 g Mono, 2.1 g Poly, 0.9 g Sat); 36 mg Cholesterol; 32 g Carbohydrate; 1 g Fibre; 4 g Protein; 221 mg Sodium

Pictured on page 53.

DATE NUT CARROT MUFFINS: Reduce all-purpose flour to 1 cup (250 mL). Add 1 cup (250 mL) whole wheat flour. Stir 1/2 cup (125 mL) chopped dates and 1/2 cup (125 mL) chopped pecans into buttermilk mixture. Bake as directed for 20 to 25 minutes.

GINGER OAT CARROT MUFFINS: Reduce all-purpose flour to 1 1/2 cups (375 mL). Add 1/2 cup (125 mL) quick-cooking rolled oats. Add 2 tsp. (10 mL) finely chopped, peeled gingerroot. Sprinkle tops of muffins with 1/4 cup (60 mL) quick-cooking rolled oats before baking. Bake as directed for 20 to 25 minutes.

Big-Batch Apple Pie Muffins

Tastes like apple pie hot from the oven! This makes a large batch of batter that can be kept refrigerated for up to one month. Bake as many as you want whenever you need hot muffins on demand!

Raisin bran cereal	5 cups	1.25 L
Large flake rolled oats	2 cups	500 mL
Boiling water	2 cups	500 mL
Cooking oil	1 cup	250 mL
Large eggs	4	4
Buttermilk	4 cups	1 L
Can of apple pie filling, chopped	19 oz.	540 mL
All-purpose flour	6 1/2 cups	1.6 L
Granulated sugar	2 cups	500 mL
Baking powder	1 tbsp.	15 mL
Baking soda	1 tbsp.	15 mL
Ground cinnamon	1 tbsp.	15 mL
Ground nutmeg	2 tsp.	10 mL
Salt	1 1/2 tsp.	7 mL

Measure first 4 ingredients into large heatproof bowl. Stir. Let stand for 5 minutes until liquid is absorbed.

Beat eggs and buttermilk in large bowl. Add pie filling. Stir. Add to cereal mixture. Stir.

Measure remaining 7 ingredients into extra-large bowl. Stir. Make a well in centre. Add cereal mixture. Stir until just moistened. Cover. Chill. Store in refrigerator for up to 1 month (see Note).

When ready to bake, fill greased muffin cups 3/4 full. Bake in 375°F (190°C) oven for 25 to 30 minutes until wooden pick inserted in centre of muffin comes out clean. Let stand in pan for 5 minutes before removing to wire rack to cool. Makes about 48 muffins.

1 muffin: 206 Calories; 6.0 g Total Fat (3.2 g Mono, 1.7 g Poly, 0.7 g Sat); 19 mg Cholesterol; 35 g Carbohydrate; 2 g Fibre; 4 g Protein; 248 mg Sodium

Pictured on page 18.

Note: Once refrigerated, be careful not to over-stir batter when spooning into muffin cups.

Mocha Chip Muffins

This good-for-you muffin made with whole-wheat flour and
cocoa provides two necessary elements: fibre and chocolate!

All-purpose flour	1 cup	250 mL
Whole wheat flour	1 cup	250 mL
Cocoa, sifted if lumpy	2 tbsp.	30 mL
Baking powder	1 1/2 tsp.	7 mL
Baking soda	1/2 tsp.	2 mL
Salt	1/4 tsp.	1 mL
Ground cinnamon	1/4 tsp.	1 mL
Large eggs	2	2
Cold espresso (see Note)	3/4 cup	175 mL
Liquid honey	1/2 cup	125 mL
Cooking oil	1/4 cup	60 mL
Unsweetened applesauce	1/4 cup	60 mL
Vanilla yogurt	1/4 cup	60 mL
Vanilla extract	1 tsp.	5 mL
Semi-sweet chocolate chips	1/2 cup	125 mL

Measure first 7 ingredients into large bowl. Stir. Make a well in centre.

Combine next 7 ingredients in medium bowl. Add to well.

Add chocolate chips. Stir until just moistened. Fill 12 greased muffin
cups almost full. Bake in 375°F (190°C) oven for 20 to 22 minutes until
wooden pick inserted in centre of muffin comes out clean. Let stand in
pan for 5 minutes before removing to wire rack to cool. Makes 12 muffins.

1 muffin: 231 Calories; 8.4 g Total Fat (4.0 g Mono, 1.8 g Poly, 2.1 g Sat); 36 mg Cholesterol;
38 g Carbohydrate; 2 g Fibre; 4 g Protein; 166 mg Sodium

Pictured on page 54.

Note: If you don't have an espresso machine, add 1 cup (250 mL) boiling
water to 3 tbsp. (50 mL) coffee grounds in mug. Let stand for 10 minutes.
Strain through fine sieve into 1 cup (250 mL) liquid measure. Cool.

Ginger Orange Muffins

*Cream cheese is used instead of butter. Subtle orange
enhances the warming flavour of ginger.*

All-purpose flour	2 cups	500 mL
Natural wheat bran	1/2 cup	125 mL
Baking soda	1 tsp.	5 mL
Baking powder	1/2 tsp.	2 mL
Ground cinnamon	1/2 tsp.	2 mL
Block of cream cheese, softened	4 oz.	125 g
Brown sugar, packed	1/2 cup	125 mL
Large eggs	2	2
Orange juice	2/3 cup	150 mL
Cooking oil	1/4 cup	60 mL
Minced crystallized ginger	1/4 cup	60 mL
Grated orange zest	1 tbsp.	15 mL

Measure first 5 ingredients into large bowl. Stir. Make a well in centre.
Set aside.

Beat cream cheese and brown sugar in medium bowl until smooth.
Add eggs 1 at a time, beating well after each addition.

Add remaining 4 ingredients. Stir. Add to well in flour mixture. Stir until
just moistened. Fill 12 greased muffin cups 3/4 full. Bake in 375°F (190°C)
oven for 18 to 20 minutes until wooden pick inserted in centre of muffin
comes out clean. Let stand in pan for 5 minutes before removing to wire
rack to cool. Makes 12 muffins.

*1 muffin: 230 Calories; 9.7 g Total Fat (4.2 g Mono, 1.8 g Poly, 2.9 g Sat); 47 mg Cholesterol;
32 g Carbohydrate; 2 g Fibre; 5 g Protein; 170 mg Sodium*

Paré Pointer
Anyone who plays with matches could make an ash of himself.

Big-Batch Walnut Muffins

Bake now or keep the batter handy in your refrigerator to bake at a moment's notice. Recipe can be easily halved if you prefer a smaller batch.

Boiling water	2 cups	500 mL
Chopped dried apricot	2 cups	500 mL
All-purpose flour	3 cups	750 mL
Whole wheat flour	3 cups	750 mL
Quick-cooking rolled oats	2 cups	500 mL
Granulated sugar	1 1/2 cups	375 mL
Baking powder	3 tbsp.	50 mL
Salt	2 tsp.	10 mL
Ground ginger	2 tsp.	10 mL
Ground cinnamon	2 tsp.	10 mL
Ground nutmeg	2 tsp.	10 mL
Large eggs	6	6
Cooking oil	1 1/2 cups	375 mL
Fancy (mild) molasses	1 1/2 cups	375 mL
Buttermilk	4 cups	1 L
Walnut halves, toasted (see Tip, page 95) and coarsely chopped	4 cups	1 L

Pour boiling water over apricot in medium heatproof bowl. Stir. Let stand for 10 minutes until softened. Drain well. Set aside.

Measure next 9 ingredients into extra-large bowl. Stir. Make a well in centre.

Beat next 4 ingredients with whisk in large bowl. Add to well.

Add walnuts and apricot. Stir until just moistened. Cover. Chill. Store in refrigerator for up to 1 month (see Note).

When ready to bake, fill greased muffin cups 3/4 full. Bake in 375°F (190°C) oven for about 20 minutes until wooden pick inserted in centre of muffin comes out clean. Let stand in pan for 5 minutes before removing to wire rack to cool. Makes about 54 muffins.

1 muffin: 243 Calories; 12.5 g Total Fat (5.3 g Mono, 5.2 g Poly, 1.3 g Sat); 25 mg Cholesterol; 30 g Carbohydrate; 2 g Fibre; 5 g Protein; 182 mg Sodium

Note: Once refrigerated, be careful not to over-stir batter when spooning into muffin cups.

Blueberry Bulgur Muffins

Large and hearty! Full of blueberry bites, with citrus and vanilla undertones.

Boiling water	1/2 cup	125 mL
Bulgur, fine grind	1/4 cup	60 mL
All-purpose flour	2 cups	500 mL
Granulated sugar	1/2 cup	125 mL
Baking powder	2 tsp.	10 mL
Baking soda	1/2 tsp.	2 mL
Ground cinnamon	1/2 tsp.	2 mL
Salt	1/4 tsp.	1 mL
Large eggs	2	2
Vanilla yogurt	1 cup	250 mL
Cooking oil	1/4 cup	60 mL
Grated lime zest	1 tsp.	5 mL
Fresh (or frozen) blueberries	1 1/2 cups	375 mL

Stir boiling water into bulgur in small heatproof bowl. Let stand for 10 minutes until liquid is absorbed. Set aside.

Measure next 6 ingredients into large bowl. Stir. Make a well in centre.

Combine next 4 ingredients in medium bowl. Add bulgur. Stir. Add to well.

Add blueberries. Stir gently just until moistened. Fill 12 greased muffin cups full. Bake in 375°F (190°C) oven for about 25 minutes until wooden pick inserted in centre of muffin comes out clean. Let stand in pan for 5 minutes before removing to wire rack to cool. Makes 12 muffins.

1 muffin: 211 Calories; 6.4 g Total Fat (3.3 g Mono, 1.7 g Poly, 0.9 g Sat); 37 mg Cholesterol; 34 g Carbohydrate; 2 g Fibre; 5 g Protein; 190 mg Sodium

 tip 2 1/2 tbsp. (37 mL) whole flaxseed may be ground in a blender or coffee grinder to yield 1/4 cup (60 mL) ground flaxseed. Use only the amount needed in the recipe. Store remaining amount in airtight container in the refrigerator.

Ground flaxseed is digested more readily than whole flaxseeds, which simply pass through the body. Grinding the seeds just before using them best preserves flavour and nutrition, but pre-ground seeds are more convenient.

Chocolate Beet Muffins

Deep, dark appearance and rich flavour result from
this unusual combination of beets and cocoa.

All-purpose flour	1 3/4 cups	425 mL
Cocoa, sifted if lumpy	1/4 cup	60 mL
Baking soda	1 tsp.	5 mL
Baking powder	1/2 tsp.	2 mL
Salt	1/2 tsp.	2 mL
Ground cinnamon	1/4 tsp.	1 mL
Butter (or hard margarine), softened	1/4 cup	60 mL
Granulated sugar	1/2 cup	125 mL
Large eggs	2	2
Can of sliced beets, drained and mashed	14 oz.	398 mL
Milk	3/4 cup	175 mL

Measure first 6 ingredients into large bowl. Stir. Make a well in centre.

Cream butter and sugar in medium bowl. Add eggs 1 at a time, beating well after each addition. Add beets and milk. Stir. Add to well. Stir until just moistened. Fill 12 greased muffin cups 3/4 full. Bake in 375°F (190°C) oven for 18 to 20 minutes until wooden pick inserted in centre of muffin comes out clean. Let stand in pan for 5 minutes before removing to wire rack to cool. Makes 12 muffins.

1 muffin: 170 Calories; 5.6 g Total Fat (1.7 g Mono, 0.4 g Poly, 3.1 g Sat); 48 mg Cholesterol; 27 g Carbohydrate; 2 g Fibre; 4 g Protein; 332 mg Sodium

Pictured at right.

1. Basic Carrot Muffins, page 46
2. Chocolate Beet Muffins, above
3. Zucchini Parmesan Muffins, page 70
4. Tart Lime Zucchini Loaf, page 96
5. Strawberry Rhubarb Muffins, page 26

Props courtesy of: Winners Stores

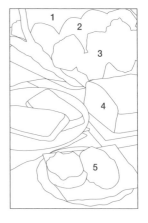

Citrus Bean Muffins

These aromatic citrus muffins are full of protein and fibre. The secret ingredient, beans, contributes more to the texture than the taste.

All-purpose flour	1 1/4 cups	300 mL
Whole wheat flour	3/4 cup	175 mL
Brown sugar, packed	1/2 cup	125 mL
Baking powder	2 tsp.	10 mL
Ground coriander	1/2 tsp.	2 mL
Salt	1/2 tsp.	2 mL
Large eggs	2	2
Canned red kidney beans, rinsed and drained	1 cup	250 mL
Orange juice	2/3 cup	150 mL
Cooking oil	1/4 cup	60 mL
Grated lemon peel	2 tsp.	10 mL

Measure first 6 ingredients into large bowl. Stir. Make a well in centre.

Process next 5 ingredients in blender or food processor until smooth. Add to well in flour mixture. Stir until just moistened. Fill 12 greased muffin cups 3/4 full. Bake in 375°F (190°C) oven for about 20 minutes until wooden pick inserted in centre of muffin comes out clean. Let stand in pan for 5 minutes before removing to wire rack to cool. Makes 12 muffins.

1 muffin: 196 Calories; 6.1 g Total Fat (3.2 g Mono, 1.7 g Poly, 0.7 g Sat); 36 mg Cholesterol; 31 g Carbohydrate; 3 g Fibre; 5 g Protein; 213 mg Sodium

Pictured at left.

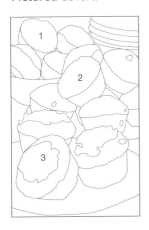

1. Citrus Bean Muffins, above
2. Mocha Chip Muffins, page 48
3. Nutty Cream Carrot Muffins, page 43

Props courtesy of: Danesco Inc.

Caribbean Muffins

Tropical flavours come together to delight your senses—coconut, mango and lime, with crunchy brazil nuts. Make these when you want to really impress!

All-purpose flour	1 cup	250 mL
Whole wheat flour	1/2 cup	125 mL
Natural oat bran	1/2 cup	125 mL
Chopped brazil nuts (or almonds), toasted (see Tip, page 95)	1/4 cup	60 mL
Baking powder	2 tsp.	10 mL
Baking soda	1/2 tsp.	2 mL
Salt	1/4 tsp.	1 mL
Packages of coconut dessert tofu (5.35 oz., 150 g, each)	2	2
Granulated sugar	1/2 cup	125 mL
Large egg	1	1
Chopped fresh (or frozen) mango	1 cup	250 mL
Mashed overripe banana (about 1 medium)	1/2 cup	125 mL
Dark (navy) rum (or 1/4 tsp., 1 mL, rum extract plus 2 tbsp., 30 mL, water)	2 tbsp.	30 mL
Lime juice	1 tbsp.	15 mL
Grated lime zest	2 tsp.	10 mL
Finely chopped brazil nuts (or almonds), toasted (see Tip, page 95)	2 tbsp.	30 mL
GLAZE		
Brown sugar, packed	1/4 cup	60 mL
Butter (or hard margarine)	1 tbsp.	15 mL
Lime juice	2 tsp.	10 mL
Dark (navy) rum (or 1/8 tsp., 0.5 mL, rum extract plus 2 tsp., 10 mL, water)	2 tsp.	10 mL

Measure first 7 ingredients into large bowl. Stir. Make a well in centre.

(continued on next page)

Muffins

Beat tofu, granulated sugar and egg in medium bowl until smooth. Add next 6 ingredients. Stir. Add to well. Stir until just moistened. Fill 12 greased muffin cups 3/4 full.

Sprinkle with second amount of brazil nuts. Bake in 375°F (190°C) oven for about 25 minutes until wooden pick inserted in centre of muffin comes out clean.

Glaze: Combine all 4 ingredients in small saucepan. Bring to a boil on medium. Heat and stir for about 1 minute until slightly thickened. Spoon over hot muffins. Let stand in pan for 5 minutes before removing to wire rack to cool. Makes 12 muffins.

1 muffin: 222 Calories; 6.2 g Total Fat (1.9 g Mono, 2.1 g Poly, 1.8 g Sat); 21 mg Cholesterol; 37 g Carbohydrate; 2 g Fibre; 6 g Protein; 189 mg Sodium

Pictured on page 71.

Apple Cheddar Muffins

Add some flaxseed and make these even healthier!

All-purpose flour	1 3/4 cups	425 mL
Granulated sugar	1/2 cup	125 mL
Ground flaxseed (see Tip, page 51)	1/4 cup	60 mL
Baking powder	1 tbsp.	15 mL
Salt	1/2 tsp.	2 mL
Ground cinnamon	1/4 tsp.	1 mL
Large egg	1	1
Grated medium Cheddar cheese	1 cup	250 mL
Apple juice	1/2 cup	125 mL
Cooking oil	1/4 cup	60 mL
Medium cooking apple (such as McIntosh), peeled and grated	1	1

Measure first 6 ingredients into large bowl. Stir. Make a well in centre.

Combine remaining 5 ingredients in medium bowl. Add to well. Stir until just moistened. Fill 12 greased muffin cups 3/4 full. Bake in 375°F (190°C) oven for 18 to 20 minutes until wooden pick inserted in centre of muffin comes out clean. Let stand in pan for 5 minutes before removing to wire rack to cool. Makes 12 muffins.

1 muffin: 222 Calories; 9.9 g Total Fat (4.2 g Mono, 2.4 g Poly, 2.7 g Sat); 28 mg Cholesterol; 28 g Carbohydrate; 1 g Fibre; 6 g Protein; 261 mg Sodium

Muffins

Upside Down Plum "Cakes"

A rosy fruit surprise bakes under spiced wheat and bran "cakes"—then becomes the crowning glory after turning them out of the pan.

Buttermilk (or soured milk, see Tip, page 13)	1 cup	250 mL
Bran flakes cereal	1 cup	250 mL
Brown sugar, packed	6 tbsp.	100 mL
Fresh red (or black) plums, with peel, pitted, thinly sliced into 12 pieces each	3	3
All-purpose flour	3/4 cup	175 mL
Whole wheat flour	3/4 cup	175 mL
Baking powder	2 tsp.	10 mL
Ground cinnamon	1 tsp.	5 mL
Ground nutmeg	1/2 tsp.	2 mL
Baking soda	1/2 tsp.	2 mL
Salt	1/4 tsp.	1 mL
Large eggs	2	2
Granulated sugar	3/4 cup	175 mL
Cooking oil	1/4 cup	60 mL
Vanilla extract	1 tsp.	5 mL

Pour buttermilk over cereal in small bowl. Let stand for 10 minutes.

Spoon 1 1/2 tsp. (7 mL) brown sugar into 12 greased muffin cups. Arrange 3 plum slices over brown sugar in each cup.

Measure next 7 ingredients into large bowl. Stir. Make a well in centre.

Combine remaining 4 ingredients in medium bowl. Add cereal mixture. Stir. Add to well. Stir until just moistened. Fill prepared muffin cups 3/4 full. Bake in 375°F (190°C) oven for 18 to 20 minutes until wooden pick inserted in centre of muffin comes out clean. Immediately run knife around inside edge of muffin cups to loosen. Invert pan onto baking sheet. Transfer any remaining plum slices in muffin cups to inverted muffins. Cool. Makes 12 muffins.

1 muffin: 219 Calories; 6.3 g Total Fat (3.3 g Mono, 1.7 g Poly, 0.8 g Sat); 37 mg Cholesterol; 38 g Carbohydrate; 2 g Fibre; 4 g Protein; 225 mg Sodium

Healthy Trail Muffins

Sweet dates and crunchy nuts packed into snack-size muffins—perfect for taking on a hike! If you like date squares, you'll love these!

Boiling water	1 cup	250 mL
Chopped pitted dates	1/2 cup	125 mL
Large flake rolled oats	3/4 cup	175 mL
Chopped pecans	1/2 cup	125 mL
All-purpose flour	1 1/4 cups	300 mL
Brown sugar, packed	3/4 cup	175 mL
Baking powder	1 1/2 tsp.	7 mL
Baking soda	1/2 tsp.	2 mL
Salt	1/2 tsp.	2 mL
Large eggs	2	2
Buttermilk (or soured milk, see Tip, page 13)	3/4 cup	175 mL
Cooking oil	3 tbsp.	50 mL
Vanilla extract	1 tsp.	5 mL

Pour boiling water over dates in medium heatproof bowl. Let stand for about 10 minutes until softened. Do not drain.

Spread rolled oats and pecans evenly in 9 x 13 inch (22 x 33 cm) pan. Bake in 350°F (175°C) oven for about 10 minutes, stirring or shaking twice, until golden. Add to dates. Stir. Set aside.

Measure next 5 ingredients into large bowl. Stir. Make a well in centre.

Combine remaining 4 ingredients in small bowl. Add to date mixture. Stir. Add to well. Stir until just moistened. Fill 12 greased muffin cups full. Bake in 375°F (190°C) oven for about 25 minutes until wooden pick inserted in centre of muffin comes out clean. Let stand in pan for 5 minutes before removing to wire rack to cool. Makes 12 muffins.

1 muffin: 237 Calories; 8.5 g Total Fat (4.7 g Mono, 2.2 g Poly, 1.0 g Sat); 36 mg Cholesterol; 37 g Carbohydrate; 2 g Fibre; 4 g Protein; 233 mg Sodium

Smoked Salmon Muffins

All the classic flavours of smoked salmon on rye toast. Chill leftovers.

All-purpose flour	1 cup	250 mL
Rye flour	1 cup	250 mL
Baking powder	1 1/2 tsp.	7 mL
Baking soda	1/2 tsp.	2 mL
Salt	1/4 tsp.	1 mL
Large eggs	2	2
Milk	3/4 cup	175 mL
Chopped smoked salmon (about 3 oz., 85 g)	1/2 cup	125 mL
Finely chopped green onion	1/2 cup	125 mL
Olive (or cooking) oil	1/4 cup	60 mL
Liquid honey	1 tbsp.	15 mL
Lemon juice	1 tbsp.	15 mL
Chopped fresh dill (or 3/4 tsp., 4 mL, dill weed)	1 tbsp.	15 mL
Grated lemon zest	1/2 tsp.	2 mL
Cream cheese, softened	1/4 cup	60 mL
Chopped fresh dill (or 3/4 tsp., 4 mL, dill weed)	1 tbsp.	15 mL
Capers, chopped (optional)	1 tsp.	5 mL
Grated lemon zest	1/2 tsp.	2 mL

Measure first 5 ingredients into large bowl. Stir. Make a well in centre.

Combine next 9 ingredients in small bowl. Add to well. Stir until just moistened. Fill 12 greased muffin cups 3/4 full.

Mash remaining 4 ingredients in small cup. Spoon about 1 tsp. (5 mL) onto centre of each muffin. Bake in 375°F (190°C) oven for 18 to 20 minutes until wooden pick inserted in centre of muffin comes out clean and tops are firm to touch. Let stand in pan for 5 minutes before removing to wire rack to cool. Makes 12 muffins.

1 muffin: 165 Calories; 8.1 g Total Fat (4.6 g Mono, 0.8 g Poly, 2.2 g Sat); 43 mg Cholesterol; 18 g Carbohydrate; 2 g Fibre; 5 g Protein; 226 mg Sodium

Pictured on page 89.

Muffins

Basic Cornmeal Muffins

A sunny yellow muffin that lends itself well to variations.
Savoury or sweet additions make these very versatile.

All-purpose flour	1 1/2 cups	375 mL
Yellow cornmeal	1 cup	250 mL
Granulated sugar	1/2 cup	125 mL
Baking powder	2 tsp.	10 mL
Baking soda	1 tsp.	5 mL
Salt	1/2 tsp.	2 mL
Large egg	1	1
Buttermilk (or soured milk, see Tip, page 13)	1 cup	250 mL
Butter (or hard margarine), melted	1/4 cup	60 mL

Measure first 6 ingredients into large bowl. Stir. Make a well in centre.

Combine remaining 3 ingredients in small bowl. Add to well. Stir until just moistened. Fill 12 greased muffin cups 3/4 full. Bake in 375°F (190°C) oven for about 15 minutes until wooden pick inserted in centre of muffin comes out clean. Let stand in pan for 5 minutes before removing to wire rack to cool. Makes 12 muffins.

1 muffin: 190 Calories; 5.1 g Total Fat (1.5 g Mono, 0.4 g Poly, 2.8 g Sat); 30 mg Cholesterol; 32 g Carbohydrate; 1 g Fibre; 4 g Protein; 338 mg Sodium

SOUTHWESTERN CORN MUFFINS: Increase all-purpose flour to 2 cups (500 mL). Add 1/8 tsp. (0.5 mL) cayenne pepper to flour mixture. Add 1/2 cup (125 mL) salsa and 1/2 cup (125 mL) kernel corn to buttermilk mixture. Fill 12 greased muffin cups full. Bake as directed for 18 to 20 minutes.

Pictured on page 72.

CHILI CHEESE CORN MUFFINS: Add 1 tsp. (5 mL) chili powder, 1 cup (250 mL) grated sharp Cheddar cheese and 1/4 cup (60 mL) finely chopped green onion to flour mixture. Fill 12 greased muffin cups full. Bake as directed for about 15 minutes.

SWEET APPLE CORN MUFFINS: Increase granulated sugar to 2/3 cup (150 mL). Add 1 cup (250 mL) grated peeled cooking apple (such as McIntosh) and 1/4 cup (60 mL) apple jelly to buttermilk mixture. Fill 12 greased muffin cups full. Bake as directed for 18 to 20 minutes.

Sun-Dried Tomato Muffins

Garlic, herb and tomato flavours in a fine-textured muffin.

All-purpose flour	2 1/2 cups	625 mL
Baking powder	1 1/2 tbsp.	25 mL
Granulated sugar	2 tbsp.	30 mL
Large eggs	2	2
Milk	1 cup	250 mL
Sun-dried tomato pesto	1/3 cup	75 mL
Butter (or hard margarine), melted	1/4 cup	60 mL
Grated havarti cheese	1/2 cup	125 mL

Measure first 3 ingredients into large bowl. Stir. Make a well in centre.

Combine next 4 ingredients in medium bowl. Add to well.

Add cheese. Stir until just moistened. Fill 12 greased muffin cups full. Bake in 375°F (190°C) oven for 18 to 20 minutes until wooden pick inserted in centre of muffin comes out clean. Let stand in pan for 5 minutes before removing to wire rack to cool. Makes 12 muffins.

1 muffin: 191 Calories; 7.2 g Total Fat (2.2 g Mono, 0.5 g Poly, 3.9 g Sat); 53 mg Cholesterol; 26 g Carbohydrate; 1 g Fibre; 6 g Protein; 248 mg Sodium

Low-Fat Corn Muffins

Wild rice adds a lot of character to the appearance and flavour.

All-purpose flour	2 cups	500 mL
Baking powder	2 tsp.	10 mL
Dry mustard	1 tsp.	5 mL
Salt	1/2 tsp.	2 mL
Sharp cold pack Cheddar cheese, cut up	1/4 cup	60 mL
Large eggs	2	2
Can of cream-style corn	10 oz.	284 mL
Cooked wild rice (about 1/3 cup, 75 mL, uncooked)	1 cup	250 mL
Frozen kernel corn, thawed	1/2 cup	125 mL
Buttermilk (or soured milk, see Tip, page 13)	1/2 cup	125 mL

(continued on next page)

Muffins

Measure first 4 ingredients into large bowl. Stir. Cut in cheese until mixture resembles coarse crumbs. Make a well in centre.

Combine next 5 ingredients in medium bowl. Add to well. Stir until just moistened. Fill 12 greased muffin cups 3/4 full. Bake in 375°F (190°C) oven for about 25 minutes until wooden pick inserted in centre of muffin comes out clean. Let stand in pan for 5 minutes before removing to wire rack to cool. Makes 12 muffins.

1 muffin: 148 Calories; 2.3 g Total Fat (0.7 g Mono, 0.4 g Poly, 0.9 g Sat); 39 mg Cholesterol; 27 g Carbohydrate; 1 g Fibre; 6 g Protein; 272 mg Sodium

Parmesan Muffins

Parmesan cheese pairs well with onion and herbs in tender, flavourful muffins. Great with soup, pasta or baked ham.

All-purpose flour	2 cups	500 mL
Grated Parmesan cheese	1/2 cup	125 mL
Baking powder	1 tbsp.	15 mL
Parsley flakes	1 tsp.	5 mL
Onion powder	1/2 tsp.	2 mL
Dried basil	1/2 tsp.	2 mL
Dried oregano	1/2 tsp.	2 mL
Salt	1/2 tsp.	2 mL
Large egg	1	1
Buttermilk (or soured milk, see Tip, page 13)	1 1/2 cups	375 mL
Butter (or hard margarine), melted	1/4 cup	60 mL
Granulated sugar	1 tbsp.	15 mL
Grated Parmesan cheese	1/2 cup	125 mL

Measure first 8 ingredients into large bowl. Stir. Make a well in centre.

Combine next 4 ingredients in medium bowl. Add to well. Stir until just moistened. Fill 12 greased muffin cups 2/3 full.

Sprinkle with second amount of Parmesan cheese. Bake in 375°F (190°C) oven for 18 to 20 minutes until wooden pick inserted in centre of muffin comes out clean. Let stand in pan for 5 minutes before removing to wire rack to cool. Makes 12 muffins.

1 muffin: 181 Calories; 7.7 g Total Fat (2.2 g Mono, 0.4 g Poly, 4.6 g Sat); 37 mg Cholesterol; 20 g Carbohydrate; 1 g Fibre; 8 g Protein; 437 mg Sodium

Spinach Corn Muffins

*Colourful green spinach and yellow cornmeal muffins
topped with a splash of orange melted cheese.*

All-purpose flour	2 cups	500 mL
Yellow cornmeal	1 cup	250 mL
Baking powder	4 tsp.	20 mL
Ground cumin	1 tsp.	5 mL
Lemon pepper	1/2 tsp.	2 mL
Salt	1/2 tsp.	2 mL
Large egg	1	1
Can of kernel corn, drained	12 oz.	341 mL
Milk	1 1/3 cups	325 mL
Box of frozen chopped spinach, thawed and squeezed dry	10 oz.	300 g
Butter (or hard margarine), melted	1/3 cup	75 mL
Grated sharp Cheddar cheese	1/3 cup	75 mL
Grated sharp Cheddar cheese	1/4 cup	60 mL

Measure first 6 ingredients into large bowl. Stir. Make a well in centre.

Combine next 5 ingredients in medium bowl. Add to well.

Add first amount of cheese. Stir until just moistened. Fill 12 greased muffin cups 3/4 full.

Sprinkle with second amount of cheese. Bake in 375°F (190°C) oven for 18 to 20 minutes until wooden pick inserted in centre of muffin comes out clean. Let stand in pan for 5 minutes before removing to wire rack to cool. Makes 12 muffins.

1 muffin: 238 Calories; 8.7 g Total Fat (2.5 g Mono, 0.6 g Poly, 5.0 g Sat); 40 mg Cholesterol; 33 g Carbohydrate; 2 g Fibre; 7 g Protein; 435 mg Sodium

Havarti Shrimp Muffins

Nutty havarti cheese and delicate shrimp are accented by fresh dill in these biscuit-like muffins. Serve with scrambled eggs for brunch or a bowl of soup for lunch. Chill leftovers.

All-purpose flour	2 cups	500 mL
Baking powder	1 1/2 tsp.	7 mL
Baking soda	1/2 tsp.	2 mL
Salt	1/2 tsp.	2 mL
Garlic powder	1/4 tsp.	1 mL
Pepper	1/4 tsp.	1 mL
Large eggs	2	2
Cooked salad shrimp	1 cup	250 mL
Grated dill (or plain) havarti cheese (see Tip, below)	1 cup	250 mL
Buttermilk (or soured milk, see Tip, page 13)	3/4 cup	175 mL
Butter (or hard margarine), melted	1/4 cup	60 mL
Chopped fresh dill (or 3/4 tsp., 4 mL, dill weed)	1 tbsp.	15 mL
Seafood cocktail sauce (optional)	1 1/2 tsp.	7 mL

Measure first 6 ingredients into large bowl. Stir. Make a well in centre.

Combine remaining 7 ingredients in large bowl. Add to well. Stir until just moistened. Fill 12 greased muffin cups 3/4 full. Bake in 375°F (190°C) oven for 18 to 20 minutes until wooden pick inserted in centre of muffin comes out clean. Let stand in pan for 5 minutes before removing to wire rack to cool. Makes 12 muffins.

1 muffin: 184 Calories; 8.0 g Total Fat (2.3 g Mono, 0.5 g Poly, 4.6 g Sat); 86 mg Cholesterol; 18 g Carbohydrate; 1 g Fibre; 9 g Protein; 376 mg Sodium

 tip   To grate soft cheese easily, place in the freezer for 15 to 20 minutes until very firm.

Roasted Garlic Muffins

Buttery sweet garlic, mellowed from the roasting,
is the dominant flavour. Warming aroma.

Small garlic bulb	1	1
Cooking oil	1 tsp.	5 mL
Chopped red onion	1/2 cup	125 mL
All-purpose flour	2 cups	500 mL
Baking powder	1 tsp.	5 mL
Baking soda	1/2 tsp.	2 mL
Salt	1/2 tsp.	2 mL
Large eggs, fork-beaten	2	2
Milk	3/4 cup	175 mL
Chopped fresh chives (or green onion)	1/2 cup	125 mL
Liquid honey	1/4 cup	60 mL
Olive (or cooking) oil	3 tbsp.	50 mL
Lemon juice	1 tbsp.	15 mL
Butter (or hard margarine), melted (optional)	3 tbsp.	50 mL
Grated Parmesan cheese (optional)	2 tbsp.	30 mL

Slice off about 1/4 inch (6 mm) from top of garlic bulb, just to expose cloves. Wrap bulb in greased foil. Bake in 375°F (190°C) oven for 45 minutes until cloves are softened. Let cool until able to handle. Squeeze out roasted cloves. Discard skins. Set aside.

Heat cooking oil in small frying pan on medium. Add red onion. Cook for about 5 minutes, stirring often, until softened. Remove from heat. Add roasted garlic. Mix well. Transfer to medium bowl.

Measure next 4 ingredients into large bowl. Stir. Make a well in centre.

Add next 6 ingredients to garlic mixture. Stir. Add to well. Stir until just moistened. Fill 12 greased muffin cups 2/3 full. Bake in 375°F (190°C) oven for about 15 minutes until wooden pick inserted in centre of muffin comes out clean.

Brush with melted butter. Sprinkle with Parmesan cheese. Let stand in pan for 5 minutes before removing to wire rack to cool. Makes 12 muffins.

1 muffin: 168 Calories; 5.1 g Total Fat (3.1 g Mono, 0.6 g Poly, 0.9 g Sat); 37 mg Cholesterol; 27 g Carbohydrate; 1 g Fibre; 4 g Protein; 203 mg Sodium

Mushroom Dill Muffins

Tender, earthy mushroom muffins enhanced with dill. Serve alongside soup or stew. Try using a mini-muffin pan for perfect little "mushrooms".

Butter (or hard margarine)	2 tsp.	10 mL
Chopped fresh white mushrooms	2 cups	500 mL
All-purpose flour	2 1/4 cups	550 mL
Baking powder	1 1/2 tsp.	7 mL
Dill weed	1 tsp.	5 mL
Baking soda	1/2 tsp.	2 mL
Pepper	1/4 tsp.	1 mL
Large eggs	2	2
Can of condensed cream of mushroom soup	10 oz.	284 mL
Butter (or hard margarine), melted	1/4 cup	60 mL
Milk	1/4 cup	60 mL
Lemon juice	2 tsp.	10 mL

Melt first amount of butter in large frying pan on medium-high. Add mushrooms. Cook for 5 to 10 minutes, stirring occasionally, until mushrooms are browned and liquid is evaporated. Cool.

Measure next 5 ingredients into large bowl. Stir. Make a well in centre.

Beat remaining 5 ingredients with whisk in medium bowl. Add to well. Add mushrooms. Stir until just moistened. Fill 12 greased muffin cups 3/4 full. Bake in 375°F (190°C) oven for 20 to 22 minutes until wooden pick inserted in centre of muffin comes out clean. Let stand in pan for 5 minutes before removing to wire rack to cool. Makes 12 muffins.

1 muffin: 177 Calories; 7.8 g Total Fat (2.1 g Mono, 1.3 g Poly, 3.8 g Sat); 49 mg Cholesterol; 22 g Carbohydrate; 1 g Fibre; 5 g Protein; 366 mg Sodium.

Asparagus Muffins

Tender-crisp bites of fresh asparagus paired with salty ham make for
a savoury delight! Serve with soup or mixed salad greens. Chill leftovers.

Fresh asparagus, trimmed	8 oz.	225 g
of tough ends		
Boiling water		
Ice water		
Olive (or cooking) oil	2 tsp.	10 mL
Chopped deli ham	1/2 cup	125 mL
All-purpose flour	2 3/4 cups	675 mL
Grated Parmesan cheese	1/2 cup	125 mL
Baking powder	1 tbsp.	15 mL
Salt	1/4 tsp.	1 mL
Pepper	1/4 tsp.	1 mL
Large eggs	2	2
Milk	3/4 cup	175 mL
Sour cream	1/3 cup	75 mL
Olive (or cooking) oil	1/3 cup	75 mL

Blanch asparagus in boiling water in medium frying pan for about
2 minutes until bright green. Drain. Immediately plunge into ice water
in large bowl. Let stand for 10 minutes until cold. Drain. Pat dry. Chop
into 1/4 inch (6 mm) pieces. Set aside.

Heat first amount of olive oil in medium frying pan on medium-high. Add
ham. Cook for about 2 minutes, stirring occasionally, until lightly browned
and crisp. Cool.

Measure next 5 ingredients into large bowl. Stir. Make a well in centre.

Beat next 4 ingredients with whisk in small bowl. Add to well. Add
asparagus and ham. Stir until just moistened. Fill 12 greased muffin
cups full. Bake in 375°F (190°C) oven for 20 to 25 minutes until wooden
pick inserted in centre of muffin comes out clean. Let stand in pan for
5 minutes before removing to wire rack to cool. Makes 12 muffins.

1 muffin: 271 Calories; 14.7 g Total Fat (8.2 g Mono, 1.4 g Poly, 4.2 g Sat); 50 mg Cholesterol;
25 g Carbohydrate; 1 g Fibre; 9 g Protein; 378 mg Sodium

Pizza Muffins

Wow, it tastes just like pizza! Kids will love these
in their lunch boxes. Great snack muffin.

All-purpose flour	2 cups	500 mL
Baking powder	1 tbsp.	15 mL
Baking soda	1/2 tsp.	2 mL
Salt	1/2 tsp.	2 mL
Dried basil	1/2 tsp.	2 mL
Dried oregano	1/2 tsp.	2 mL
Garlic powder	1/2 tsp.	2 mL
Large egg	1	1
Milk	1 cup	250 mL
Cooking oil	1/4 cup	60 mL
Granulated sugar	2 tbsp.	30 mL
Roma (plum) tomato, quartered, seeded, diced	1	1
Grated medium Cheddar cheese	2/3 cup	150 mL
Sliced green onion	1/4 cup	60 mL
Deli pepperoni sticks, thinly sliced (about 3/4 cup, 175 mL)	2 1/2 oz.	70 g

Measure first 7 ingredients into large bowl. Stir. Make a well in centre.

Combine next 4 ingredients in medium bowl. Add to well.

Add tomato, cheese, onion and about 1/2 cup (125 mL) pepperoni to well. Stir until just moistened. Fill 12 greased muffin cups 3/4 full. Press remaining slices of pepperoni on top of batter. Bake in 375°F (190°C) oven for about 20 minutes until a wooden pick inserted in centre of muffin comes out clean. Let stand in pan for 5 minutes before removing to wire rack to cool. Makes 12 muffins.

1 muffin: 206 Calories; 10.5 g Total Fat (5.0 g Mono, 1.9 g Poly, 3.0 g Sat); 30 mg Cholesterol; 21 g Carbohydrate; 1 g Fibre; 7 g Protein; 423 mg Sodium

Pictured on page 36.

Zucchini Parmesan Muffins

Here's the perfect solution for all that zucchini growing in the garden. Moist zucchini muffins with savoury Parmesan cheese, garlic and a hint of sage.

All-purpose flour	2 cups	500 mL
Grated Parmesan cheese	1/2 cup	125 mL
Granulated sugar	1 tbsp.	15 mL
Baking powder	1 tbsp.	15 mL
Baking soda	1/2 tsp.	2 mL
Ground sage	1/2 tsp.	2 mL
Salt	1/2 tsp.	2 mL
Garlic powder	1/4 tsp.	1 mL
Large eggs	2	2
Grated unpeeled zucchini	1 1/2 cups	375 mL
Buttermilk (or soured milk, see Tip, page 13)	3/4 cup	175 mL
Cooking oil	1/4 cup	60 mL
Worcestershire sauce	1/2 tsp.	2 mL

Measure first 8 ingredients into large bowl. Stir. Make a well in centre.

Combine next 5 ingredients in medium bowl. Add to well. Stir until just moistened. Fill 12 greased muffin cups 3/4 full. Bake in 375°F (190°C) oven for about 20 minutes until wooden pick inserted in centre of muffin comes out clean. Let stand in pan for 5 minutes before removing to wire rack to cool. Makes 12 muffins.

1 muffin: 169 Calories; 7.4 g Total Fat (3.6 g Mono, 1.7 g Poly, 1.6 g Sat); 40 mg Cholesterol; 20 g Carbohydrate; 1 g Fibre; 6 g Protein; 358 mg Sodium

Pictured on page 53.

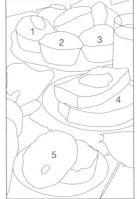

1. Basic Banana Muffins, page 24
2. Mango Muffins, page 23
3. Lemon Coconut Muffins, page 14
4. Tropical Zucchini Loaf, page 95
5. Caribbean Muffins, page 56

Lentil Pepper Muffins

Rich orange colour. Roasted red pepper, cilantro
and lentils lend Middle Eastern flair.

All-purpose flour	2 cups	500 mL
Granulated sugar	1 tbsp.	15 mL
Baking powder	2 tsp.	10 mL
Baking soda	1/2 tsp.	2 mL
Ground cumin	1/2 tsp.	2 mL
Salt	1/4 tsp.	1 mL
Large eggs	2	2
Tomato juice	1 cup	250 mL
Canned lentils, rinsed and drained	1 cup	250 mL
Roasted red pepper spreadable cream cheese	1/2 cup	125 mL
Cooking oil	2 tbsp.	30 mL
Chopped fresh cilantro or parsley	2 tbsp.	30 mL

Measure first 6 ingredients into large bowl. Stir. Make a well in centre.

Process remaining 6 ingredients in blender or food processor until smooth. Add to well. Stir until just moistened. Fill 12 greased muffin cups 3/4 full. Bake in 375°F (190°C) oven for 20 to 22 minutes until wooden pick inserted in centre of muffin comes out clean. Let stand in pan for 5 minutes before removing to wire rack to cool. Makes 12 muffins.

1 muffin: 165 Calories; 5.5 g Total Fat (2.3 g Mono, 1.0 g Poly, 1.6 g Sat); 42 mg Cholesterol; 23 g Carbohydrate; 2 g Fibre; 6 g Protein; 367 mg Sodium

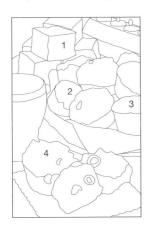

1. Jalapeño Cheese Cornbread, page 109
2. Guacamole Muffins, page 75
3. Southwestern Corn Muffins, page 61
4. Chipotle Olive Muffins, page 78

Props courtesy of: Danesco Inc.

Blue Cheese Pear Muffins

Blue cheese muffin with mellow bites of pear.

All-purpose flour	2 1/2 cups	625 mL
Baking powder	1 tbsp.	15 mL
Salt	1/2 tsp.	2 mL
Large eggs	3	3
Reserved juice from pears	3/4 cup	175 mL
Cooking oil	1/2 cup	125 mL
Milk	1/4 cup	60 mL
Can of pear halves, drained and juice reserved, chopped	14 oz.	398 mL
Pecan pieces, toasted (see Tip, page 95)	3/4 cup	175 mL
Blue cheese, crumbled	3 oz.	85 g

Measure first 3 ingredients into large bowl. Stir. Make a well in centre.

Combine next 4 ingredients in medium bowl. Add to well.

Add remaining 3 ingredients. Stir until just moistened. Fill 12 greased muffin cups full. Bake in 375°F (190°C) oven for about 25 minutes until wooden pick inserted in centre of muffin comes out clean. Let stand in pan for 5 minutes before removing to wire rack to cool. Makes 12 muffins.

1 muffin: 301 Calories; 18.5 g Total Fat (10.0 g Mono, 4.5 g Poly, 2.9 g Sat); 59 mg Cholesterol; 28 g Carbohydrate; 2 g Fibre; 7 g Protein; 311 mg Sodium

Pictured on page 89.

Cheddar Cayenne Muffins

The perfect companion for fresh garden salad or tomato soup.

All-purpose flour	2 cups	500 mL
Baking powder	1 tbsp.	15 mL
Salt	1/2 tsp.	2 mL
Cayenne pepper	1/4 tsp.	1 mL
Large egg	1	1
Milk	1 cup	250 mL
Cooking oil	1/4 cup	60 mL

(continued on next page)

Granulated sugar	2 tbsp.	30 mL
Dijon mustard	1 tbsp.	15 mL
Grated sharp Cheddar cheese	1 cup	250 mL

Measure first 4 ingredients into large bowl. Stir. Make a well in centre.

Combine next 5 ingredients in medium bowl. Add to well.

Add cheese. Stir until just moistened. Fill 12 greased muffin cups 3/4 full. Bake in 375°F (190°C) oven for 18 to 20 minutes until wooden pick inserted in centre of muffin comes out clean. Let stand in pan for 5 minutes before removing to wire rack to cool. Makes 12 muffins.

1 muffin: 188 Calories; 9.1 g Total Fat (4.0 g Mono, 1.7 g Poly, 2.8 g Sat); 29 mg Cholesterol; 20 g Carbohydrate; 1 g Fibre; 6 g Protein; 287 mg Sodium

Guacamole Muffins

The ultimate Tex-Mex muffin. Tastes like corn chips dipped in guacamole.

All-purpose flour	2 cups	500 mL
Yellow cornmeal	1 cup	250 mL
Granulated sugar	2 tbsp.	30 mL
Baking powder	2 tsp.	10 mL
Baking soda	1 tsp.	5 mL
Salt	1/2 tsp.	2 mL
Large egg	1	1
Mashed avocado	1 cup	250 mL
Medium salsa	1/2 cup	125 mL
Milk	1/3 cup	75 mL
Butter (or hard margarine), melted	1/4 cup	60 mL
Lime juice	1 tbsp.	15 mL

Measure first 6 ingredients into large bowl. Stir. Make a well in centre.

Combine remaining 6 ingredients in medium bowl. Add to well. Stir until just combined. Fill 12 greased muffin cups full. Bake in 375°F (190°C) oven for 20 to 22 minutes until wooden pick inserted in centre of muffin comes out clean. Let stand in pan for 5 minutes before removing to wire rack to cool. Makes 12 muffins.

1 muffin: 214 Calories; 8.1 g Total Fat (3.4 g Mono, 0.8 g Poly, 3.3 g Sat); 29 mg Cholesterol; 31 g Carbohydrate; 2 g Fibre; 5 g Protein; 350 mg Sodium

Pictured on page 72.

Muffins

Masa Taco Muffins

Masa harina is a corn flour used to make tortillas. It is available in most grocery stores and adds an authentic Mexican flavour. Chill leftovers.

Cooking oil	1 tsp.	5 mL
Lean ground beef	1/2 lb.	225 g
Chopped onion	1/2 cup	125 mL
Chopped green pepper	1/2 cup	125 mL
Taco seasoning	1 tbsp.	15 mL
All-purpose flour	2/3 cup	150 mL
Masa harina	2/3 cup	150 mL
Grated sharp Cheddar cheese	1/2 cup	125 mL
Yellow cornmeal	1/3 cup	75 mL
Granulated sugar	1/4 cup	60 mL
Baking powder	1 tbsp.	15 mL
Taco seasoning	1 tbsp.	15 mL
Large eggs	2	2
Milk	2/3 cup	150 mL
Mild salsa	1/4 cup	60 mL
Butter (or hard margarine), melted	2 tbsp.	30 mL
Grated sharp Cheddar cheese	1/2 cup	125 mL

Heat cooking oil in medium frying pan on medium. Add beef, onion and green pepper. Scramble-fry for about 10 minutes until beef is no longer pink. Sprinkle with first amount of taco seasoning. Heat and stir to blend flavours. Drain. Set aside.

Measure next 7 ingredients into large bowl. Stir. Make a well in centre.

Combine next 4 ingredients in medium bowl. Add to well. Add beef mixture. Stir just until moistened. Fill 12 greased muffin cups 3/4 full.

Sprinkle with second amount of cheese. Bake in 375°F (190°C) oven for 18 to 20 minutes until wooden pick inserted in centre of muffin comes out clean. Let stand in pan for 5 minutes before removing to wire rack. Serve warm. Makes 12 muffins.

1 muffin: 202 Calories; 8.7 g Total Fat (2.9 g Mono, 0.6 g Poly, 4.4 g Sat); 62 mg Cholesterol; 22 g Carbohydrate; 1 g Fibre; 9 g Protein; 332 mg Sodium

Pictured on page 36

Caramelized Onion Muffins

Sweet onion and basil are good partners for smoked cheese. Rich, delicious and hard to resist!

Cooking oil	1 tbsp.	15 mL
Thinly sliced onion	2 cups	500 mL
Brown sugar, packed	1/4 cup	60 mL
Balsamic vinegar	1 tbsp.	15 mL
Salt	1/4 tsp.	1 mL
Pepper	1/4 tsp.	1 mL
All-purpose flour	2 1/2 cups	625 mL
Grated smoked Cheddar cheese	2/3 cup	150 mL
Chopped fresh basil	3 tbsp.	50 mL
Baking powder	1 tbsp.	15 mL
Paprika	1 tsp.	5 mL
Salt	1/4 tsp.	1 mL
Large egg	1	1
Buttermilk (or soured milk, see Tip, page 13)	1 1/4 cups	300 mL
Cooking oil	1/3 cup	75 mL
Grated smoked Cheddar cheese	1/3 cup	75 mL

Heat first amount of cooking oil in large frying pan on medium. Add onion. Cook for about 15 minutes, stirring often, until caramelized.

Add next 4 ingredients. Heat and stir until brown sugar is dissolved. Cool to room temperature.

Measure next 6 ingredients into large bowl. Stir. Make a well in centre.

Combine next 3 ingredients in small bowl. Add to well. Add caramelized onion. Stir until just moistened. Fill 12 greased muffin cups full.

Sprinkle with second amount of cheese. Bake in 375°F (190°C) oven for 18 to 20 minutes until wooden pick inserted in centre of muffin comes out clean. Let stand in pan for 5 minutes before removing to wire rack to cool. Makes 12 muffins.

1 muffin: 241 Calories; 10.7 g Total Fat (5.3 g Mono, 2.5 g Poly, 2.3 g Sat); 26 mg Cholesterol; 30 g Carbohydrate; 1 g Fibre; 6 g Protein; 270 mg Sodium

Chipotle Olive Muffins

Smoky chipotle pepper heat permeates these soft,
moist muffins. A hint of lime is the perfect accent.

All-purpose flour	2 cups	500 mL
Granulated sugar	1 tbsp.	15 mL
Baking powder	1 1/2 tsp.	7 mL
Baking soda	1 tsp.	5 mL
Salt	1/2 tsp.	2 mL
Large eggs	2	2
Sour cream	1 cup	250 mL
Grated Monterey Jack cheese	1 cup	250 mL
Chipotle chili peppers in adobo sauce, chopped (see Tip, below)	2	2
Can of sliced black olives, drained	4 1/2 oz.	125 mL
Cooking oil	1/4 cup	60 mL
Grated lime zest	1 tsp.	5 mL

Measure first 5 ingredients into large bowl. Stir. Make a well in centre.

Combine remaining 7 ingredients in medium bowl. Add to well. Stir until just moistened. Fill 12 greased muffin cups 3/4 full. Bake in 375°F (190°C) oven for 18 to 20 minutes until wooden pick inserted in centre of muffin comes out clean. Let stand in pan for 5 minutes before removing to wire rack to cool. Makes 12 muffins.

1 muffin: 215 Calories; 12.1 g Total Fat (5.2 g Mono, 1.9 g Poly, 4.4 g Sat); 53 mg Cholesterol; 20 g Carbohydrate; 1 g Fibre; 7 g Protein; 500 mg Sodium

Pictured on page 72.

 tip Chipotle chili peppers are smoked jalapeño peppers. Be sure to wash your hands after handling. To store any leftover chipotle chili peppers, divide into recipe-friendly portions and freeze, with sauce, in airtight containers for up to one year.

Potato Asiago Muffins

Add that last bit of leftover mashed potatoes to these
dumpling-like muffins. Nutmeg, dill and cheese expand the flavour.

All-purpose flour	1 3/4 cups	425 mL
Granulated sugar	1 tbsp.	15 mL
Baking powder	1 tbsp.	15 mL
Baking soda	1/2 tsp.	2 mL
Salt	1/2 tsp.	2 mL
Ground nutmeg	1/4 tsp.	1 mL
Large eggs	2	2
Mashed potatoes (about 8 oz., 225 g, cooked)	3/4 cup	175 mL
Buttermilk (or soured milk, see Tip, page 13)	1 1/4 cups	300 mL
Butter (or hard margarine), melted	2 tbsp.	30 mL
Chopped fresh dill (or 3/4 tsp., 4 mL, dill weed)	1 tbsp.	15 mL
Grated Asiago cheese	1/2 cup	125 mL

Measure first 6 ingredients into large bowl. Stir. Make a well in centre.

Beat remaining 6 ingredients with whisk in medium bowl. Add to well.
Stir until just moistened. Fill 12 greased muffin cups 3/4 full. Bake in 375°F
(190°C) oven for 20 to 22 minutes until wooden pick inserted in centre of
muffin comes out clean. Let stand in pan for 5 minutes before removing to
wire rack to cool. Makes 12 muffins.

1 muffin: 139 Calories; 4.4 g Total Fat (1.3 g Mono, 0.3 g Poly, 2.3 g Sat); 46 mg Cholesterol;
20 g Carbohydrate; 1 g Fibre; 5 g Protein; 324 mg Sodium

Paré Pointer

Their best baseball player is a piano tuner. He has a perfect pitch.

Loaves

For all its rustic, homespun appearance, a good loaf can be the centrepiece of any table. Put it on an attractive cutting board, cut the first few slices and watch everyone gather round. To ensure your loaf is a star attraction, please read the Tips for Terrific Quick Breads on page 8, and consider these points:

- While it's irresistible to serve when it's hot, a loaf that is sliced once it's cooled for several hours (or even overnight) crumbles less. A serrated knife is useful for the job.

- Not all loaf pans are the same size. We used a 9 x 5 x 3 inch (22 x 125 x 7.5 cm) loaf pan, but if you're using smaller ones and have too much batter, make muffins with the leftovers. Fill empty muffin cups with 1/4 inch (6 mm) water to prevent your tin from buckling in the heat. Be careful when removing the muffin tin from the oven as the water will be hot.

- Loaves are ideal for bake sales and fundraisers. If you're using smaller pans, the temperature stays the same but the cooking time will lessen. Loaves in disposable foil pans also need less time than loaves in regular pans of the same size. Be careful when you put disposable pans into the oven—they can collapse if lifted from the sides. Support them from underneath.

Favourite Lemon Loaf

Light and buttery with a delicate lemon flavour.
A perfect match for vanilla ice cream.

All-purpose flour	2 cups	500 mL
Baking powder	1 1/4 tsp.	6 mL
Salt	1/2 tsp.	2 mL
Butter (or hard margarine), softened	1/2 cup	125 mL
Granulated sugar	1 cup	250 mL
Large eggs	3	3
Milk	1/2 cup	125 mL
Grated lemon zest	1 1/2 tbsp.	25 mL
GLAZE		
Lemon juice	1/4 cup	60 mL
Icing (confectioner's) sugar	1/4 cup	60 mL

(continued on next page)

Loaves

Measure first 3 ingredients into medium bowl. Stir. Set aside.

Cream butter and sugar in large bowl. Add eggs 1 at a time, beating well after each addition.

Add flour mixture in 3 parts, alternating with milk in 2 parts, stirring after each addition until just combined. Add lemon zest. Stir until just combined. Spread in greased 9 x 5 x 3 inch (22 x 12.5 x 7.5 cm) loaf pan. Bake in 325°F (160°C) oven for about 1 hour until wooden pick inserted in centre comes out clean.

Glaze: Stir lemon juice into icing sugar in small bowl until smooth. Randomly poke several holes in loaf with wooden pick. Spoon lemon juice mixture over hot loaf. Let stand in pan until cooled completely. Cuts into 16 slices.

1 slice: 192 Calories; 7.3 g Total Fat (2.2 g Mono, 0.4 g Poly, 4.2 g Sat); 57 mg Cholesterol; 29 g Carbohydrate; 1 g Fibre; 3 g Protein; 181 mg Sodium

LEMON BLUEBERRY LOAF: Fold in 1 cup (250 mL) fresh (or frozen) blueberries when adding zest until just combined. Bake as directed for 60 to 65 minutes.

LEMON POPPY SEED LOAF: Add 2 tbsp. (30 mL) poppy seeds to flour mixture. Bake as directed.

Paré Pointer

After the thief fell into some wet cement,
he became a hardened criminal.

Butterscotch Pumpkin Loaf

Candied butterscotch topping makes this spiced pumpkin loaf extra special.

All-purpose flour	2 cups	500 mL
Brown sugar, packed	1/2 cup	125 mL
Baking powder	2 tsp.	10 mL
Ground cinnamon	1 tsp.	5 mL
Ground nutmeg	1/2 tsp.	2 mL
Baking soda	1/2 tsp.	2 mL
Salt	1/2 tsp.	2 mL
Large egg	1	1
Milk	1/2 cup	125 mL
Butter (or hard margarine), melted	1/4 cup	60 mL
Canned pure pumpkin (no spices), (see Tip, page 83)	1 cup	250 mL
Butterscotch chips	1 cup	250 mL
Chopped pecans	1/2 cup	125 mL
Butterscotch (or caramel) ice cream topping	1/4 cup	60 mL

Measure first 7 ingredients into large bowl. Stir. Make a well in centre.

Beat next 4 ingredients with whisk in medium bowl. Add to well.

Add butterscotch chips and pecans. Stir until just moistened. Spread in greased 9 x 5 x 3 inch (22 x 12.5 x 7.5 cm) loaf pan.

Drizzle with ice cream topping. Bake in 350°F (175°C) oven for about 1 hour until wooden pick inserted in centre comes out clean. Let stand in pan for 10 minutes. Run knife around loaf to loosen before removing to wire rack to cool. Cuts into 16 slices.

1 slice: 229 Calories; 9.7 g Total Fat (3.8 g Mono, 1.0 g Poly, 4.3 g Sat); 25 mg Cholesterol; 33 g Carbohydrate; 1 g Fibre; 4 g Protein; 233 mg Sodium

Pictured on front cover.

Mincemeat Nut Bread

Moist, flavourful loaf with mincemeat and walnuts generously dispersed throughout. A wonderful pumpkin spice flavour.

All-purpose flour	2 cups	500 mL
Ground cinnamon	1 1/2 tsp.	7 mL
Baking powder	1 tsp.	5 mL
Baking soda	1 tsp.	5 mL
Salt	1/2 tsp.	2 mL
Butter (or hard margarine), softened	2/3 cup	150 mL
Granulated sugar	1 cup	250 mL
Large eggs	2	2
Mincemeat	1 cup	250 mL
Canned pure pumpkin (no spices), (see Tip, below)	1 cup	250 mL
Coarsely chopped walnuts	3/4 cup	175 mL

Measure first 5 ingredients into large bowl. Stir. Make a well in centre. Set aside.

Cream butter and sugar in medium bowl. Add eggs 1 at a time, beating well after each addition.

Add remaining 3 ingredients. Stir. Add to well in flour mixture. Stir until just moistened. Spread in greased 9 × 5 × 3 inch (22 × 12.5 × 7.5 cm) loaf pan. Bake in 350°F (175°C) oven for about 1 hour until wooden pick inserted in centre comes out clean. Let stand in pan for 10 minutes before removing to wire rack to cool. Cuts into 16 slices.

1 slice: 271 Calories; 12.8 g Total Fat (3.4 g Mono, 2.8 g Poly, 5.5 g Sat); 49 mg Cholesterol; 37 g Carbohydrate; 1 g Fibre; 4 g Protein; 305 mg Sodium

Pictured on page 107.

 tip Store any leftover pumpkin in an airtight container in the refrigerator for 3 to 5 days or in the freezer for up to 12 months.

Cranberry Streusel Loaf

Buttery pound cake texture with tart bites of cranberry
and crunchy streusel topping. Perfect for coffee breaks.

All-purpose flour	2 cups	500 mL
Brown sugar, packed	3/4 cup	175 mL
Baking powder	1 1/2 tsp.	7 mL
Salt	1 tsp.	5 mL
Large eggs	2	2
Butter (or hard margarine), melted	1/2 cup	125 mL
Buttermilk (or soured milk, see Tip, page 13)	3/4 cup	175 mL
Vanilla extract	1 1/2 tsp.	7 mL
Grated lemon zest	1 tsp.	5 mL
Dried cranberries, chopped	1 cup	250 mL
TOPPING		
Finely chopped walnuts	1/4 cup	60 mL
Brown sugar, packed	2 tbsp.	30 mL
Ground cinnamon	1/4 tsp.	1 mL

Measure first 4 ingredients into large bowl. Stir. Make a well in centre.

Combine next 5 ingredients in medium bowl. Add to well.

Add cranberries. Stir until just moistened. Spread in greased 9 × 5 × 3 inch (22 × 12.5 × 7.5 cm) loaf pan.

Topping: Combine all 3 ingredients in small bowl. Sprinkle on batter. Bake in 350°F (175°C) oven for 45 to 50 minutes until wooden pick inserted in centre comes out clean. Let stand in pan for 10 minutes before removing to wire rack to cool. Cuts into 16 slices.

1 slice: 202 Calories; 8.2 g Total Fat (2.3 g Mono, 1.2 g Poly, 4.2 g Sat); 44 mg Cholesterol; 29 g Carbohydrate; 2 g Fibre; 4 g Protein; 271 mg Sodium

Pictured on page 90.

Chocolate Brownie Loaf

Cocoa not only makes this loaf delicious—it also adds fibre! Drizzle the brownie-like loaf with fresh strawberry or raspberry coulis.

Butter (or hard margarine)	1/4 cup	60 mL
Cocoa, sifted if lumpy	1/3 cup	75 mL
Granulated sugar	3/4 cup	175 mL
Large egg, fork-beaten	1	1
Milk	1 cup	250 mL
Vanilla extract	1 tsp.	5 mL
All-purpose flour	2 cups	500 mL
Baking powder	2 tsp.	10 mL
Baking soda	1 tsp.	5 mL
Salt	1/2 tsp.	2 mL
Semi-sweet chocolate chips	1 cup	250 mL

Combine butter and cocoa in small saucepan. Heat and stir on medium until melted and smooth. Remove from heat. Add sugar. Stir. Add egg. Mix well.

Add milk and vanilla. Stir.

Measure next 4 ingredients into large bowl. Stir. Make a well in centre. Add chocolate mixture to well.

Add chocolate chips. Stir until just moistened. Spread in greased 9 x 5 x 3 inch (22 x 12.5 x 7.5 cm) loaf pan. Bake in 350°F (175°C) oven for about 50 minutes until wooden pick inserted in centre comes out clean. Let stand in pan for 10 minutes before removing to wire rack to cool. Cuts into 16 slices.

1 slice: 196 Calories; 7.3 g Total Fat (2.3 g Mono, 0.4 g Poly, 4.3 g Sat); 22 mg Cholesterol; 32 g Carbohydrate; 2 g Fibre; 4 g Protein; 246 mg Sodium

Pictured on page 35.

Mango Coconut Bread

The lemon enhances the naturally sweet flavours of mango and coconut.

Cans of sliced mango in syrup (14 oz., 398 mL, each), drained and syrup reserved	2	2
All-purpose flour	1 3/4 cups	425 mL
Medium unsweetened coconut	2/3 cup	150 mL
Pecan pieces, toasted (see Tip, page 95) and chopped	1/2 cup	125 mL
Baking powder	2 1/2 tsp.	12 mL
Salt	1/4 tsp.	1 mL
Butter (or hard margarine), softened	1/3 cup	75 mL
Granulated sugar	2/3 cup	150 mL
Lemon juice	2 tbsp.	30 mL
Large eggs	2	2
GLAZE		
Reserved syrup from mango slices	3/4 cup	175 mL
Granulated sugar	1/4 cup	60 mL
Lemon juice	1 tbsp.	15 mL

Process mango in blender until smooth. Set aside.

Measure next 5 ingredients into large bowl. Stir. Make a well in centre.

Cream butter and first amounts of sugar and lemon juice in small bowl. Add eggs 1 at a time, beating well after each addition. Add mango. Stir. Add to well. Stir until just moistened. Spread in greased 9 x 5 x 3 inch (22 x 12.5 x 7.5 cm) loaf pan. Bake in 350°F (175°C) oven for about 1 hour until wooden pick inserted in centre comes out clean.

Glaze: Combine all 3 ingredients in small saucepan on medium. Heat and stir until boiling and sugar is dissolved. Boil for 5 minutes, stirring occasionally, until slightly thickened. Pour evenly over hot loaf. Let stand in pan for 10 minutes before removing to wire rack to cool. Cuts into 16 slices.

1 slice: 242 Calories; 10.1 g Total Fat (3.2 g Mono, 1.0 g Poly, 5.2 g Sat); 38 mg Cholesterol; 37 g Carbohydrate; 1 g Fibre; 3 g Protein; 157 mg Sodium

Chai Pumpkin Loaf

Mild chai tea flavours complement pumpkin. Pumpkin seeds add lots of crunch.

All-purpose flour	2 cups	500 mL
Baking powder	2 tsp.	10 mL
Baking soda	1 tsp.	5 mL
Salt	1/4 tsp.	1 mL
Butter (or hard margarine), softened	1/4 cup	60 mL
Brown sugar, packed	1/2 cup	125 mL
Large eggs	2	2
Canned pure pumpkin (no spices), (see Tip, page 83)	1 cup	250 mL
Chai tea concentrate	1 cup	250 mL
Raw pumpkin seeds	3/4 cup	175 mL

Measure first 4 ingredients into large bowl. Stir. Make a well in centre. Set aside.

Cream butter and brown sugar in medium bowl. Add eggs 1 at a time, beating well after each addition.

Add remaining 3 ingredients. Stir. Add to well in flour mixture. Stir until just moistened. Spread in greased 9 × 5 × 3 inch (22 × 12.5 × 7.5 cm) loaf pan. Bake in 350°F (175°C) oven for 55 to 60 minutes until wooden pick inserted in centre comes out clean. Let stand in pan for 10 minutes before removing to wire rack to cool. Cuts into 16 slices.

1 slice: 172 Calories; 7.1 g Total Fat (2.1 g Mono, 1.7 g Poly, 2.8 g Sat); 35 mg Cholesterol; 24 g Carbohydrate; 2 g Fibre; 4 g Protein; 208 mg Sodium

Paré Pointer
Naturally, fortune tellers dance at the crystal ball.

Orange Poppy Seed Loaf

A twist to the familiar lemon poppy seed loaf. Lots of poppy seeds and fresh orange flavour. This will become a favourite.

All-purpose flour	2 cups	500 mL
Poppy seeds	2 tbsp.	30 mL
Baking powder	2 tsp.	10 mL
Baking soda	1/2 tsp.	2 mL
Salt	1/2 tsp.	2 mL
Butter (or hard margarine), softened	1/3 cup	75 mL
Granulated sugar	3/4 cup	175 mL
Large eggs	2	2
Sour cream	3/4 cup	175 mL
Orange juice	1/2 cup	125 mL
Grated orange zest	1 tbsp.	15 mL
Vanilla extract	1 1/2 tsp.	7 mL

Measure first 5 ingredients into large bowl. Stir. Make a well in centre. Set aside.

Cream butter and sugar in medium bowl. Add eggs 1 at a time, beating well after each addition.

Add remaining 4 ingredients. Stir. Add to well in flour mixture. Stir until just moistened. Spread in greased 9 x 5 x 3 inch (22 x 12.5 x 7.5 cm) loaf pan. Bake in 350°F (175°C) oven for about 50 minutes until wooden pick inserted in centre comes out clean. Let stand in pan for 10 minutes before removing to wire rack to cool. Cuts into 16 slices.

1 slice: 172 Calories; 6.9 g Total Fat (2.0 g Mono, 0.7 g Poly, 3.8 g Sat); 42 mg Cholesterol; 24 g Carbohydrate; 1 g Fibre; 3 g Protein; 215 mg Sodium

1. Blue Cheese Pear Muffins, page 74
2. Smoked Salmon Muffins, page 60
3. Mediterranean Tomato Loaf, page 104

Props courtesy of: Canhome Global
Cherison Enterprises Inc.

Quick Ginger Molasses Loaf

Dress up this bundt pan loaf with a sprinkle of icing sugar.

All-purpose flour	2 cups	500 mL
Ground flaxseed (see Tip, page 51)	1/4 cup	60 mL
Ground ginger	2 tsp.	10 mL
Ground cinnamon	2 tsp.	10 mL
Baking powder	1 1/2 tsp.	7 mL
Baking soda	1/2 tsp.	2 mL
Ground cloves	1/2 tsp.	2 mL
Salt	1/2 tsp.	2 mL
Large eggs	2	2
Pitted prunes	3/4 cup	175 mL
Fancy (mild) molasses	3/4 cup	175 mL
Buttermilk (or soured milk, see Tip, page 13)	3/4 cup	175 mL
Brown sugar, packed	1/2 cup	125 mL
Cooking oil	1/4 cup	60 mL
Minced crystallized ginger	3 tbsp.	50 mL

Measure first 8 ingredients into large bowl. Stir. Make a well in centre.

Process remaining 7 ingredients in blender or food processor until smooth. Add to well. Stir until just moistened. Spread in greased 12 cup (3 L) bundt pan. Bake in 350°F (175°C) oven for 45 to 50 minutes until wooden pick inserted in centre comes out clean. Let stand in pan for 10 minutes before removing to wire rack to cool. Cuts into 16 slices.

1 slice: 216 Calories; 5.5 g Total Fat (2.6 g Mono, 1.8 g Poly, 0.6 g Sat); 27 mg Cholesterol; 40 g Carbohydrate; 2 g Fibre; 4 g Protein; 182 mg Sodium

1. Cranberry Streusel Loaf, page 84
2. Blueberry Nut Loaf, page 94
3. Spinach Feta Loaf, page 103
4. Bacon Beer Bread, page 102
5. Sunshine Bread, page 101

Props courtesy of: Cherison Enterprises Inc.

Mocha Swirl Loaf

Pretty swirls with chunks of chocolate. With the delicious
glaze on top, this cake-like loaf is ideal for tea time.

All-purpose flour	2 cups	500 mL
Baking powder	2 tsp.	10 mL
Baking soda	1/2 tsp.	2 mL
Ground cinnamon	1/2 tsp.	2 mL
Salt	1/4 tsp.	1 mL
Butter (or hard margarine), softened	1/2 cup	125 mL
Granulated sugar	1 cup	250 mL
Large eggs	2	2
Sour cream	3/4 cup	175 mL
Vanilla extract	1 tsp.	5 mL
Semi-sweet chocolate baking squares (1 oz., 28 g, each), chopped	2	2
Instant coffee granules, crushed to fine powder	2 tsp.	10 mL
GLAZE		
Coffee-flavoured liqueur	2 tbsp.	30 mL
Icing (confectioner's) sugar	1/2 cup	125 mL

Measure first 5 ingredients into large bowl. Stir. Make a well in centre.

Cream butter and sugar in medium bowl. Add eggs 1 at a time, beating well after each addition.

Add sour cream and vanilla. Stir. Add to well. Stir until just moistened. Remove 1/2 of batter to small bowl. Set aside.

Add chocolate and coffee to remaining batter. Stir until just combined. Add reserved batter. Fold once. Spread in greased 9 x 5 x 3 inch (22 x 12.5 x 7.5 cm) loaf pan. Bake in 350°F (175°C) oven for about 50 minutes until wooden pick inserted in centre comes out clean. Let stand in pan for 10 minutes before removing to wire rack to cool.

Glaze: Stir liqueur into icing sugar in small bowl until smooth. Drizzle over loaf. Cuts into 16 slices.

1 slice: 233 Calories; 9.5 g Total Fat (2.8 g Mono, 0.5 g Poly, 5.6 g Sat); 48 mg Cholesterol; 34 g Carbohydrate; 1 g Fibre; 3 g Protein; 199 mg Sodium

Basic Banana Bread

Be sure to use overripe bananas for best results.

All-purpose flour	2 cups	500 mL
Baking soda	1 tsp.	5 mL
Salt	1/2 tsp.	2 mL
Butter (or hard margarine), softened	1/2 cup	125 mL
Granulated sugar	1 cup	250 mL
Large eggs	2	2
Mashed overripe banana (about 3 medium)	1 1/2 cups	375 mL
Lemon juice	1 tbsp.	15 mL
Vanilla extract	1 tsp.	5 mL

Measure first 3 ingredients into large bowl. Stir. Make a well in centre. Set aside.

Cream butter and sugar in medium bowl. Add eggs 1 at a time, beating well after each addition.

Add remaining 3 ingredients. Stir. Add to well in flour mixture. Stir until just moistened. Spread in greased 9 x 5 x 3 inch (22 x 12.5 x 7.5 cm) loaf pan. Bake in 350°F (175°C) oven for 55 to 60 minutes until wooden pick inserted in centre comes out clean. Let stand in pan for 10 minutes before removing to wire rack to cool. Cuts into 16 slices.

1 slice: 196 Calories; 7.0 g Total Fat (2.0 g Mono, 0.4 g Poly, 4.1 g Sat); 43 mg Cholesterol; 31 g Carbohydrate; 1 g Fibre; 3 g Protein; 225 mg Sodium

Pictured on page 17.

GRANOLA BANANA BREAD: Add 1/2 cup (125 mL) granola to flour mixture. Add 1/2 cup (125 mL) dark raisins and 1/2 cup (125 mL) chopped walnuts to batter. Sprinkle 1/3 cup (75 mL) granola on loaf before baking. Bake as directed for 60 to 70 minutes.

Pictured on page 17.

CHOCOLATE KISSED BANANA BREAD: Add 1 cup (250 mL) chopped milk chocolate kisses to batter. Bake as directed.

Pictured on page 17.

SKINNY MONKEY BREAD: Reduce butter (or hard margarine) to 1/4 cup (60 mL). Reduce sugar to 1/3 cup (75 mL). Increase mashed banana to 2 cups (500 mL). Bake as directed.

Blueberry Nut Loaf

Plenty of hazelnut crunch and blueberry bites in this big loaf.

All-purpose flour	2 1/2 cups	625 mL
Hazelnuts (filberts), toasted (see Tip, page 95), skinned (see Note), coarsely chopped	1 cup	250 mL
Minced crystallized ginger	1/4 cup	60 mL
Baking powder	1 tbsp.	15 mL
Salt	1/4 tsp.	1 mL
Butter (or hard margarine), softened	1/2 cup	125 mL
Brown sugar, packed	1 cup	250 mL
Large egg	1	1
Buttermilk (or soured milk see Tip, page 13)	1 cup	250 mL
Fresh (or frozen) blueberries	1 cup	250 mL
TOPPING		
Butter (or hard margarine), melted	2 tbsp.	30 mL
Coarse brown sugar (such as Sugar in the Raw)	3 tbsp.	50 mL
Quick-cooking rolled oats	2 tbsp.	30 mL

Measure first 5 ingredients into large bowl. Stir. Make a well in centre.

Cream butter and brown sugar in small bowl. Add egg. Beat well. Add buttermilk. Stir. Add to well. Stir until just moistened. Gently fold in blueberries. Spread in greased 9 x 5 x 3 inch (22 x 12.5 x 7.5 cm) loaf pan.

Topping: Combine all 3 ingredients in separate small bowl. Sprinkle on batter. Bake in 350°F (175°C) oven for about 1 hour until wooden pick inserted in centre comes out clean. Let stand in pan for 10 minutes before removing to wire rack to cool. Cuts into 16 slices.

1 slice: 284 Calories; 13.4 g Total Fat (6.4 g Mono, 0.9 g Poly, 5.3 g Sat); 34 mg Cholesterol; 38 g Carbohydrate; 1 g Fibre; 4 g Protein; 213 mg Sodium

Pictured on page 90.

Note: To peel hazelnuts, spread toasted nuts on half of tea towel. Fold other half over nuts. Press down and rub vigorously for 1 to 2 minutes, until almost all skins are removed. You may not be able to remove all skins from the hazelnuts, but the outer paper skins should come off.

Tropical Zucchini Loaf

Moist and delicious—the perfect choice for a buffet table or a sweet snack.

All-purpose flour	2 cups	500 mL
Baking soda	1 tsp.	5 mL
Baking powder	1/2 tsp.	2 mL
Ground cinnamon	1/4 tsp.	1 mL
Ground allspice	1/8 tsp.	0.5 mL
Ground cloves	1/8 tsp.	0.5 mL
Large eggs	2	2
Granulated sugar	1 cup	250 mL
Cooking oil	1/3 cup	75 mL
Vanilla extract	1 tsp.	5 mL
Salt	1/2 tsp.	2 mL
Can of crushed pineapple, drained	14 oz.	398 mL
Grated unpeeled zucchini	1 cup	250 mL
Medium sweetened coconut	1/2 cup	125 mL

Measure first 6 ingredients into large bowl. Stir. Make a well in centre.

Combine next 5 ingredients in medium bowl until smooth.

Add remaining 3 ingredients. Stir. Add to well. Stir until just moistened. Spread in greased 9 × 5 × 3 inch (22 × 12.5 × 7.5 cm) loaf pan. Bake in 350°F (175°C) oven for about 1 hour until wooden pick inserted in centre comes out clean. Let stand in pan for 10 minutes before removing to wire rack to cool. Cuts into 16 slices.

1 slice: 185 Calories; 6.4 g Total Fat (3.1 g Mono, 1.6 g Poly, 1.3 g Sat); 27 mg Cholesterol; 30 g Carbohydrate; 1 g Fibre; 3 g Protein; 181 mg Sodium

Pictured on page 71.

 tip To toast nuts, seeds or coconut, place them in an ungreased shallow frying pan. Heat on medium for 3 to 5 minutes, stirring often, until golden. To bake, spread them evenly in an ungreased shallow pan. Bake in a 350°F (175°C) oven for 5 to 10 minutes, stirring or shaking often, until golden.

Tart Lime Zucchini Loaf

A very unique variation of the traditional zucchini loaf. The green flecks of zucchini look just like bits of lime. Great the next day as the tart flavour mellows upon standing.

All-purpose flour	1 1/2 cups	375 mL
Bran buds cereal	1 cup	250 mL
Baking powder	2 tsp.	10 mL
Baking soda	1 tsp.	5 mL
Ground cinnamon	1 tsp.	5 mL
Salt	1/2 tsp.	2 mL
Ground nutmeg	1/4 tsp.	1 mL
Large eggs	2	2
Granulated sugar	1/3 cup	75 mL
Brown sugar, packed	1/3 cup	75 mL
Cooking oil	1/3 cup	75 mL
Vanilla extract	1 tsp.	5 mL
Grated unpeeled zucchini	2 cups	500 mL
Grated lime zest	1 tbsp.	15 mL
GLAZE		
Lime juice	1/4 cup	60 mL
Granulated sugar	1/4 cup	60 mL

Measure first 7 ingredients into large bowl. Stir. Make a well in centre.

Beat next 5 ingredients with whisk in medium bowl. Add to well.

Add zucchini and lime zest. Stir until just moistened. Spread in greased 9 x 5 x 3 inch (22 x 12.5 x 7.5 cm) loaf pan. Bake in 350°F (175°C) oven for about 50 minutes until wooden pick inserted in centre comes out clean.

Glaze: Stir lime juice into sugar in small cup until sugar is dissolved. Randomly poke several holes in loaf with wooden pick. Spoon lime juice mixture over loaf. Let stand in pan until cooled completely. Cuts into 16 slices.

1 slice: 165 Calories; 5.7 g Total Fat (3.1 g Mono, 1.6 g Poly, 0.6 g Sat); 27 mg Cholesterol; 28 g Carbohydrate; 3 g Fibre; 3 g Protein; 250 mg Sodium

Pictured on page 53.

Herb Beer Bread

Italian herbs and beer flavour this moist, tender loaf.
Try a slice toasted and spread with garlic butter.

All-purpose flour	2 cups	500 mL
Whole wheat flour	3/4 cup	175 mL
Grated Parmesan cheese	1/2 cup	125 mL
Wheat germ	1/4 cup	60 mL
Baking powder	4 tsp.	20 mL
Granulated sugar	1 tbsp.	15 mL
Italian seasoning	2 tsp.	10 mL
Salt	1/2 tsp.	2 mL
Can of beer (room temperature)	12 1/2 oz.	355 mL
Melted butter	3 tbsp.	50 mL

Measure first 8 ingredients into large bowl. Stir. Make a well in centre.

Add beer and butter to well. Stir until just moistened. Spread in greased 9 x 5 x 3 inch (22 x 12.5 x 7.5 cm) loaf pan. Bake in 350°F (175°C) oven for about 50 minutes until wooden pick inserted in centre comes out clean. Let stand in pan for 10 minutes before removing to wire rack to cool. Cuts into 16 slices.

1 slice: 136 Calories; 3.6 g Total Fat (1.0 g Mono, 0.3 g Poly, 2.1 g Sat); 9 mg Cholesterol; 20 g Carbohydrate; 2 g Fibre; 4 g Protein; 301 mg Sodium

---

Paré Pointer
To see an iceberg many miles away, you need good ice sight.

Trail Mix Loaf

Packed full of whole foods—make this your energy bar for the next nature hike.

Ingredient	Imperial	Metric
Boiling water	3/4 cup	175 mL
Fancy (mild) molasses	2 tbsp.	30 mL
Quick-cooking rolled oats	1/4 cup	60 mL
Natural wheat bran	1/4 cup	60 mL
All-purpose flour	1/2 cup	125 mL
Brown sugar, packed	1/3 cup	75 mL
Whole wheat flour	1/4 cup	60 mL
Baking powder	1 tsp.	5 mL
Baking soda	1/2 tsp.	2 mL
Salt	1/2 tsp.	2 mL
Large egg	1	1
Buttermilk (or soured milk, see Tip, page 13)	1/4 cup	60 mL
Unsweetened applesauce	1/4 cup	60 mL
Cooking oil	2 tbsp.	30 mL
Vanilla extract	1 tsp.	5 mL
Chopped walnuts (or pecans)	1/4 cup	60 mL
Salted, roasted sunflower seeds	1/4 cup	60 mL
Dark raisins	1/4 cup	60 mL
Chopped pitted dates	1/4 cup	60 mL
Chopped dried apricot	1/4 cup	60 mL
Medium unsweetened coconut	1/4 cup	60 mL

Stir boiling water into molasses in medium heatproof bowl. Add rolled oats and bran. Stir. Let stand for 10 minutes.

Measure next 6 ingredients into large bowl. Stir. Make a well in centre.

Combine next 5 ingredients in small bowl. Add to rolled oats mixture. Stir. Add to well.

Add remaining 6 ingredients. Stir until just moistened. Line bottom of greased 9 x 5 x 3 inch (22 x 12.5 x 7.5 cm) loaf pan with waxed paper. Spread batter in pan. Bake in 350°F (175°C) oven for about 50 minutes until wooden pick inserted in centre comes out clean. Let stand in pan for 10 minutes before removing to wire rack to cool. Cuts into 16 slices.

1 slice: 135 Calories; 5.6 g Total Fat (1.7 g Mono, 2.2 g Poly, 1.3 g Sat); 14 mg Cholesterol; 20 g Carbohydrate; 2 g Fibre; 3 g Protein; 167 mg Sodium

Pumpernickel Loaf

Rye loaf sweetened with molasses. Use thin slices for sandwiches.

All-purpose flour	1 1/2 cups	375 mL
Rye flour	1 1/4 cups	300 mL
Wheat germ	1/4 cup	60 mL
Cocoa, sifted if lumpy	1 tbsp.	15 mL
Baking powder	2 tsp.	10 mL
Baking soda	1/2 tsp.	2 mL
Salt	1/2 tsp.	2 mL
Large eggs	2	2
Plain yogurt	1 1/2 cups	375 mL
Fancy (mild) molasses	1/4 cup	60 mL
Butter (or hard margarine), melted	3 tbsp.	50 mL

Measure first 7 ingredients into large bowl. Stir. Make a well in centre.

Combine remaining 4 ingredients in medium bowl. Add to well. Stir until just moistened. Spread in greased 9 × 5 × 3 inch (22 × 12.5 × 7.5 cm) loaf pan. Bake in 350°F (175°C) oven for 50 to 60 minutes until wooden pick inserted in centre comes out clean. Let stand in pan for 10 minutes before removing to wire rack to cool. Cuts into 16 slices.

1 slice: 141 Calories; 3.7 g Total Fat (1.0 g Mono, 0.4 g Poly, 1.9 g Sat); 34 mg Cholesterol; 23 g Carbohydrate; 2 g Fibre; 5 g Protein; 211 mg Sodium

Paré Pointer
That farmer was really cross. Somebody got his goat.

Moroccan Spice Loaf

All the exotic flavours of a couscous salad baked into
this moist, compact loaf. Sweet bites of currant and
crunchy pistachios. Try with curry chicken or lentil soup.

All-purpose flour	1 1/2 cups	375 mL
Brown sugar, packed	2 tbsp.	30 mL
Baking powder	2 tsp.	10 mL
Baking soda	1/2 tsp.	2 mL
Ground coriander	1/2 tsp.	2 mL
Ground cumin	1/2 tsp.	2 mL
Ground ginger	1/2 tsp.	2 mL
Salt	1/2 tsp.	2 mL
Ground cinnamon	1/4 tsp.	1 mL
Chili powder	1/4 tsp.	1 mL
Boiling water	2/3 cup	150 mL
Couscous	1/2 cup	125 mL
Large egg, fork-beaten	1	1
Milk	2/3 cup	150 mL
Cooking oil	1/4 cup	60 mL
Lemon juice	2 tbsp.	30 mL
Chopped pistachios	1/2 cup	125 mL
Currants	1/4 cup	60 mL
Sliced green onion	3 tbsp.	50 mL

Measure first 10 ingredients into large bowl. Stir. Make a well in centre. Set aside.

Pour boiling water over couscous in medium heatproof bowl. Stir. Cover. Let stand for 5 minutes until water is absorbed. Fluff with fork.

Add next 4 ingredients. Stir. Add to well in flour mixture.

Add remaining 3 ingredients. Stir until just moistened. Spread in greased 9 x 5 x 3 inch (22 x 12.5 x 7.5 cm) loaf pan. Bake in 350°F (175°C) oven for about 45 minutes until wooden pick inserted in centre comes out clean. Let stand in pan for 10 minutes before removing to wire rack to cool. Cuts into 16 slices.

1 slice: 150 Calories; 6.5 g Total Fat (3.8 g Mono, 1.5 g Poly, 0.7 g Sat); 14 mg Cholesterol; 20 g Carbohydrate; 1 g Fibre; 4 g Protein; 173 mg Sodium

Sunshine Bread

Lots of nuts, lots of texture. Toast a slice of this sunny
yellow bread to go with your favourite soup or stew.

All-purpose flour	1 cup	250 mL
Whole wheat flour	1/2 cup	125 mL
Yellow cornmeal	1/2 cup	125 mL
Wheat germ	1/4 cup	60 mL
Ground flaxseed (see Tip, page 51)	1/4 cup	60 mL
Granulated sugar	2 tbsp.	30 mL
Baking powder	1 tbsp.	15 mL
Turmeric	1/2 tsp.	2 mL
Salt	1/2 tsp.	2 mL
Large egg	1	1
Milk	3/4 cup	175 mL
Unsweetened applesauce	1/2 cup	125 mL
Cooking oil	2 tbsp.	30 mL
Roasted, salted sunflower seeds	1/3 cup	75 mL
Flaxseed	1 tbsp.	15 mL

Measure first 9 ingredients into large bowl. Stir. Make a well in centre.

Combine next 4 ingredients in medium bowl. Add to well.

Add sunflower seeds. Stir until just moistened. Spread in greased
9 x 5 x 3 inch (22 x 12.5 x 7.5 cm) loaf pan.

Sprinkle with flaxseed. Bake in 350°F (175°C) oven for about 40 minutes
until wooden pick inserted in centre comes out clean. Let stand in pan for
10 minutes before removing to wire rack to cool. Cuts into 16 slices.

1 slice: 134 Calories; 5.0 g Total Fat (1.7 g Mono, 2.4 g Poly, 0.6 g Sat); 14 mg Cholesterol;
19 g Carbohydrate; 2 g Fibre; 4 g Protein; 178 mg Sodium

Pictured on page 90.

Bacon Beer Bread

Experiment with different types of beer to modify the flavour and colour. A dense, compact loaf. Chill leftovers.

Bacon slices, diced	6	6
All-purpose flour	1 3/4 cups	425 mL
Masa harina (see Note)	3/4 cup	175 mL
Granulated sugar	2 tbsp.	30 mL
Baking powder	1 tbsp.	15 mL
Chili powder	1 tsp.	5 mL
Salt	1/2 tsp.	2 mL
Can of dark beer (room temperature)	12 1/2 oz.	355 mL
Finely sliced green onion	1/4 cup	60 mL
Grated medium Cheddar cheese	1/4 cup	60 mL

Cook bacon in small frying pan on medium until crisp. Drain, reserving 2 tbsp. (30 mL) drippings in small cup. Set aside.

Measure next 6 ingredients into large bowl. Stir. Make a well in centre.

Add beer, onion, bacon and drippings to well. Stir until just moistened. Spread in greased 9 x 5 x 3 inch (22 x 12.5 x 7.5 cm) loaf pan.

Sprinkle with cheese. Bake in 350°F (175°C) oven for about 40 minutes until wooden pick inserted in centre comes out clean. Let stand in pan for 10 minutes before removing to wire rack to cool. Cuts into 16 slices.

1 slice: 126 Calories; 3.8 g Total Fat (1.5 g Mono, 0.5 g Poly, 1.5 g Sat); 6 mg Cholesterol; 18 g Carbohydrate; 1 g Fibre; 3 g Protein; 197 mg Sodium

Pictured on page 90.

Note: Masa harina is a corn flour traditionally used to make tortillas. Masa harina is available in the baking aisle of most grocery stores.

Spinach Feta Loaf

This unusual-looking loaf will win you rave reviews. Salty feta is the perfect contrast to sweet raisins and earthy spinach. A great way to get the family to eat spinach!

All-purpose flour	2 cups	500 mL
Baking powder	1 tbsp.	15 mL
Baking soda	1 tsp.	5 mL
Salt	1/4 tsp.	1 mL
Pepper	1/4 tsp.	1 mL
Butter (or hard margarine), softened	1/3 cup	75 mL
Granulated sugar	1/2 cup	125 mL
Large eggs	2	2
Box of frozen chopped spinach, thawed and squeezed dry	10 oz.	300 g
Milk	2/3 cup	150 mL
Crumbled feta cheese	1 cup	250 mL
Dark raisins	1/2 cup	125 mL

Measure first 5 ingredients into large bowl. Stir. Make a well in centre.

Cream butter and sugar in small bowl. Add eggs 1 at a time, beating well after each addition. Add spinach and milk. Stir. Add to well.

Add cheese and raisins. Stir until just moistened. Spread in greased 9 x 5 x 3 inch (22 x 12.5 x 7.5 cm) loaf pan. Bake in 350°F (175°C) oven for 55 to 60 minutes until wooden pick inserted in centre comes out clean. Let stand in pan for 10 minutes before removing to wire rack to cool. Cuts into 16 slices.

1 slice: 183 Calories; 7.2 g Total Fat (1.9 g Mono, 0.4 g Poly, 4.4 g Sat); 47 mg Cholesterol; 25 g Carbohydrate; 1 g Fibre; 5 g Protein; 368 mg Sodium

Pictured on page 90.

Paré Pointer

A man-eating tiger escaped. No threat to women and children.

Mediterranean Tomato Loaf

Wonderful flavours of the Mediterranean—sun-dried tomatoes, basil, oregano and feta cheese. Make sure to refrigerate the leftovers, if there are any! Very attractive when cut.

All-purpose flour	2 cups	500 mL
Granulated sugar	1 tbsp.	15 mL
Baking powder	1 1/2 tsp.	7 mL
Baking soda	1 tsp.	5 mL
Coarse ground pepper	1/2 tsp.	2 mL
Large eggs	2	2
Tomato juice	1 cup	250 mL
Ricotta cheese	3/4 cup	175 mL
Crumbled feta cheese	1/2 cup	125 mL
Sun-dried tomatoes in oil, blotted dry, chopped	1/2 cup	125 mL
Cooking oil	1/4 cup	60 mL
Chopped fresh oregano	1/4 cup	60 mL
Chopped fresh basil	2 tbsp.	30 mL
Large basil leaves (optional)	4	4
Oil from sun-dried tomatoes	1 1/2 tsp.	7 mL

Measure first 5 ingredients into large bowl. Stir. Make a well in centre.

Combine next 8 ingredients in medium bowl. Add to well. Stir until just moistened. Spread in greased 9 × 5 × 3 inch (22 × 12.5 × 7.5 cm) loaf pan.

Arrange basil leaves on top. Brush with oil from sun-dried tomatoes. Bake in 350°F (175°C) oven for about 50 minutes until wooden pick inserted in centre comes out clean. Let stand in pan for 10 minutes before removing to wire rack to cool. Cuts into 16 slices.

1 slice: 151 Calories; 7.6 g Total Fat (3.4 g Mono, 1.4 g Poly, 2.3 g Sat); 38 mg Cholesterol; 16 g Carbohydrate; 1 g Fibre; 5 g Protein; 259 mg Sodium

Pictured on page 89.

Irish Soda Bread

Over the years, this recipe has been changed and modernized to the muffin-like texture that is most common today. Serve with soup or stew.

All purpose flour	4 cups	1 L
Granulated sugar	1/3 cup	75 mL
Baking soda	2 tsp.	10 mL
Salt	1 tsp.	5 mL
Cold butter (or hard margarine), cut up	1/4 cup	60 mL
Buttermilk (or soured milk, see Tip, page 13)	2 cups	500 mL
All-purpose flour	1 – 2 tbsp.	15 – 30 mL

Combine first 4 ingredients in large bowl. Cut in butter until mixture resembles coarse crumbs. Make a well in centre.

Add buttermilk to well. Stir until almost combined. Turn out onto lightly floured surface. Sprinkle dough with second amount of flour if necessary to prevent sticking. Knead 8 to 10 times until soft dough forms. Transfer to greased 9 inch (22 cm) round pan. Press or pat out to within 1/2 inch (12 mm) of pan edge. Let stand for 5 minutes. Cut "+" on top of dough, about 1/2 inch (12 mm) deep and 5 inches (12.5 cm) across, using sharp knife. Bake in 350°F (175°C) oven for 45 to 50 minutes until wooden pick inserted in centre comes out clean. Let stand in pan for 10 minutes before removing to wire rack to cool. Cuts into 16 slices.

1 slice: 179 Calories; 3.7 g Total Fat (1.0 g Mono, 0.3 g Poly, 2.1 g Sat); 9 mg Cholesterol; 32 g Carbohydrate; 1 g Fibre; 5 g Protein; 375 mg Sodium

BROWN SODA BREAD: Reduce all-purpose flour to 2 cups (500 mL). Add 2 cups (500 mL) whole wheat flour. Add 1/4 cup (60 mL) fancy (mild) molasses when adding buttermilk. Bake as directed.

POLKA DOT SODA BREAD: Add 1/2 cup (125 mL) raisins to well in flour mixture. Bake as directed.

ROSEMARY SODA BREAD: Increase sugar to 1/2 cup (125 mL). Add 1 cup (250 mL) toasted pine nuts and 2 tsp. (10 mL) chopped fresh rosemary to well in flour mixture. Bake as directed for 50 to 60 minutes.

Blue Cheese Walnut Loaf

Mild blue cheese goes well with crunchy toasted walnuts.
Try a slice of this with spinach salad or cream soup.

All-purpose flour	2 cups	500 mL
Granulated sugar	1/4 cup	60 mL
Seasoned salt	1 1/4 tsp.	6 mL
Baking powder	1 tsp.	5 mL
Baking soda	1/2 tsp.	2 mL
Large eggs	2	2
Buttermilk (or soured milk, see Tip, page 13)	1 cup	250 mL
Crumbled blue cheese	1/4 cup	60 mL
Cooking oil	2 tbsp.	30 mL
Grated mozzarella cheese	1 cup	250 mL
Chopped walnuts, toasted, (see Tip, page 95)	1/4 cup	60 mL

Measure first 5 ingredients into large bowl. Stir. Make a well in centre.

Combine next 4 ingredients in medium bowl. Add to well.

Add mozzarella cheese and walnuts. Stir until just moistened. Spread in greased 9 x 5 x 3 inch (22 x 12.5 x 7.5 cm) loaf pan. Bake in 350°F (175°C) oven for 45 to 50 minutes until wooden pick inserted in centre comes out clean. Let stand in pan for 10 minutes before removing to wire rack to cool. Cuts into 16 slices.

1 slice: 147 Calories; 6.2 g Total Fat (2.3 g Mono, 1.5 g Poly, 2.0 g Sat); 35 mg Cholesterol; 17 g Carbohydrate; 1 g Fibre; 6 g Protein; 242 mg Sodium

1. Apple Mince Muffins, page 13
2. Rummy Eggnog Muffins, page 31
3. Orange Pumpkin Muffins, page 12
4. Mincemeat Nut Bread, page 83
5. Spiced Fruit Muffins, page 20

Props courtesy of: Cherison Enterprises Inc.

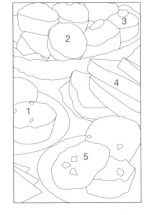

Jalapeño Cheese Cornbread

Moist cornbread with the perfect amount of jalepeño heat.

All-purpose flour	1 1/2 cups	375 mL
Yellow cornmeal	1 cup	250 mL
Granulated sugar	1/4 cup	60 mL
Baking powder	2 tsp.	10 mL
Baking soda	1/2 tsp.	2 mL
Salt	1/2 tsp.	2 mL
Grated jalapeño Monterey Jack cheese	1 cup	250 mL
Large eggs, fork-beaten	2	2
Buttermilk (or soured milk, see Tip, page 13)	1 cup	250 mL
Butter (or hard margarine), melted	1/2 cup	125 mL
Can of sliced jalapeño peppers, drained and chopped	4 oz.	114 mL

Combine first 6 ingredients in large bowl. Add cheese. Stir. Make a well in centre.

Combine remaining 4 ingredients in medium bowl. Add to well. Stir until just moistened. Spread in greased 8 x 8 inch (20 x 20 cm) pan. Bake in 350°F (175°C) oven for about 35 minutes until wooden pick inserted in centre comes out clean. Cuts into 9 pieces.

1 piece: 338 Calories; 16.7 g Total Fat (4.9 g Mono, 0.9 g Poly, 9.8 g Sat); 90 mg Cholesterol; 38 g Carbohydrate; 2 g Fibre; 9 g Protein; 587 mg Sodium

Pictured on page 72.

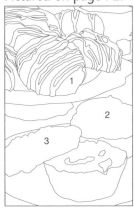

1. Cinnamon Swirls, page 111
2. Lemon Yogurt Muffins, page 22
3. Raspberry Muffins, page 28

Props courtesy of: Cherison Enterprises Inc.

Biscuits & Scones

Biscuits dunked into gravy, a fragrant scone tucked in beside a teacup—these wonderful quick breads transform the ordinary into special occasions. To make sure your scones (rhymes with lawns, not loans) and biscuits are a success, read the Tips for Terrific Quick Breads on page 8. The following hints are specific to biscuits and scones:

- Use a pastry blender to cut the butter just until it's the size of small peas or large crumbs. This size is important, as it allows the pastry to flake. The butter must be cold.

- Cut your shapes by putting the biscuit cutter straight into the dough. Don't twist the cutter in the dough, as this will result in lopsided biscuits.

- Once you've finished cutting, follow the advice of the baker's man and "pat-a-cake" by gently patting the scraps together to cut again. Don't re-roll the dough, as it will toughen. If you can no longer use the cutter because there isn't enough dough left, create other shapes—triangles or rectangles—with a knife.

- For fast biscuits, roll your dough into a square and cut it into smaller squares, rectangles or triangles. This way, there's no waste and no need to reshape.

- For soft-sided biscuits, place them close together on the baking sheet. Put them further apart for crisper results.

- Finally, when a recipe asks you to score your scones, it has nothing to do with a rating system (though your family might give them a perfect 10!). Scoring means making shallow cuts in the dough with a sharp knife. This stops the dough from cracking randomly since the dough can now expand in the cuts.

110

Cinnamon Swirls

Dough is quite tender, so use waxed paper to help with the rolling.

All-purpose flour	1 1/2 cups	375 mL
Granulated sugar	2 tbsp.	30 mL
Baking powder	2 tsp.	10 mL
Baking soda	1/4 tsp.	1 mL
Salt	1/2 tsp.	2 mL
Cold butter (or hard margarine), cut up	1/4 cup	60 mL
Sour cream	3/4 cup	175 mL
Butter (or hard margarine), melted	1 1/2 tbsp.	25 mL
Granulated sugar	2 tbsp.	30 mL
Ground cinnamon	1 tsp.	5 mL
ICING		
Icing (confectioner's) sugar	1/2 cup	125 mL
Milk	1 tbsp.	15 mL
Ground cinnamon	1/8 tsp.	0.5 mL

Combine first 5 ingredients in large bowl. Cut in butter until mixture resembles coarse crumbs. Make a well in centre.

Add sour cream to well. Stir until soft dough forms. Turn out onto lightly floured surface. Gently knead 4 or 5 times until dough just comes together. Gently roll out on waxed paper on dampened work surface to 8 x 12 inch (20 x 30 cm) rectangle. Brush dough with melted butter, leaving 1 inch (2.5 cm) edge on 1 long side.

Combine second amount of granulated sugar and cinnamon in small cup. Sprinkle on top of butter. Roll up from covered long side, jelly-roll style, using waxed paper as guide. Pinch seam against roll to seal. Cut into 1 inch (2.5 cm) slices, using floured knife. Lay slices flat, about 1 1/2 inches (3.8 cm) apart, on greased baking sheet. Bake in 400°F (205°C) oven for about 15 minutes until golden. Let stand on baking sheet for 5 minutes before removing to wire rack.

Icing: Combine all 3 ingredients in small bowl until smooth. Drizzle over swirls. Makes 12 swirls.

1 swirl: 171 Calories; 7.9 g Total Fat (2.2 g Mono, 0.4 g Poly, 4.8 g Sat); 21 mg Cholesterol; 23 g Carbohydrate; 1 g Fibre; 2 g Protein; 252 mg Sodium

Pictured on page 108 and on back cover.

Raisin Oatcakes

These little "cakes" are perfect for afternoon tea with a dollop of berry jam.

All-purpose flour	1 1/2 cups	375 mL
Quick-cooking rolled oats	1 cup	250 mL
Granulated sugar	1/4 cup	60 mL
Baking powder	1 tbsp.	15 mL
Salt	1/2 tsp.	2 mL
Cold butter (or hard margarine), cut up	1/2 cup	125 mL
Large egg, fork-beaten	1	1
Milk	2/3 cup	150 mL
Golden raisins	1/2 cup	125 mL

Combine first 5 ingredients in large bowl. Cut in butter until mixture resembles coarse crumbs. Make a well in centre.

Add remaining 3 ingredients to well. Stir until soft dough forms. Turn out onto lightly floured surface. Knead 8 times. Roll or pat out to 1/2 inch (12 mm) thickness. Cut out circles with lightly floured 2 inch (5 cm) biscuit cutter. Arrange about 1/2 inch (12 mm) apart on greased baking sheet. Bake in 400°F (205°C) oven for 12 to 15 minutes until golden. Let stand on baking sheet for 5 minutes before removing to wire rack. Makes about 24 oatcakes.

1 oatcake: 107 Calories; 4.7 g Total Fat (1.4 g Mono, 0.3 g Poly, 2.7 g Sat); 20 mg Cholesterol; 15 g Carbohydrate; 1 g Fibre; 2 g Protein; 144 mg Sodium

Paré Pointer
Borrow some eggs, borrow some butter,
borrow some sugar, and make a sponge cake.

Low-Fat Pesto Biscuits

Sun-dried tomato pesto lends a robust herb flavour—super with soup!

All-purpose flour	2 1/2 cups	625 mL
Baking powder	1 tbsp.	15 mL
Granulated sugar	2 tsp.	10 mL
Salt	1/2 tsp.	2 mL
Large egg	1	1
Mashed potatoes	1/2 cup	125 mL
Milk	1/2 cup	125 mL
Butter (or hard margarine), melted	2 tbsp.	30 mL
Sun-dried tomato (or basil) pesto	2 tbsp.	30 mL

Combine first 4 ingredients in large bowl. Make a well in centre.

Beat remaining 5 ingredients with whisk in medium bowl. Add to well. Stir until soft dough forms. Turn out onto lightly floured surface. Knead 8 times. Roll or pat out to 1/2 inch (12 mm) thickness. Cut out circles with lightly floured 2 inch (5 cm) biscuit cutter. Arrange about 1 inch (2.5 cm) apart on greased baking sheet. Bake in 400°F (205°C) oven for about 15 minutes until golden. Let stand on baking sheet for 5 minutes before removing to wire rack. Makes 18 biscuits.

1 biscuit: 95 Calories; 2.0 g Total Fat (0.6 g Mono, 0.2 g Poly, 1.0 g Sat); 16 mg Cholesterol; 16 g Carbohydrate; 1 g Fibre; 3 g Protein; 151 mg Sodium

Paré Pointer
Knock, knock. Who's there? Gladys. Gladys who?
Gladys not me the wolf wants for dinner.

Basic Buttermilk Biscuits

Buttery biscuits. Brush tops with buttermilk, milk or melted butter for browner tops. Delicious served with softly whipped cream, jam and fresh berries.

All-purpose flour	2 cups	500 mL
Baking powder	2 tsp.	10 mL
Baking soda	1/2 tsp.	2 mL
Salt	1/2 tsp.	2 mL
Cold butter (or hard margarine), cut up	1/4 cup	60 mL
Buttermilk (or soured milk, see Tip, page 13)	3/4 cup	175 mL

Combine first 4 ingredients in large bowl. Cut in butter until mixture resembles coarse crumbs. Make a well in centre.

Add buttermilk to well. Stir until soft dough forms. Turn out onto lightly floured surface. Knead 8 times. Roll or pat out to 1/2 inch (12 mm) thickness. Cut out circles with lightly floured 2 inch (5 cm) biscuit cutter. Arrange about 1 inch (2.5 cm) apart on greased baking sheet. Bake in 400°F (205°C) oven for about 15 minutes until golden. Let stand on baking sheet for 5 minutes before removing to wire rack. Makes about 18 biscuits.

1 biscuit: 82 Calories; 3.0 g Total Fat (0.8 g Mono, 0.2 g Poly, 1.8 g Sat); 8 mg Cholesterol; 12 g Carbohydrate; trace Fibre; 2 g Protein; 182 mg Sodium

Pictured on page 125.

ORANGE CARDAMOM BISCUITS: Add 2 tbsp. (30 mL) granulated sugar and 1/2 tsp. (2 mL) ground cardamom to flour mixture. Add 1 tbsp. (15 mL) grated orange zest to buttermilk before adding to flour mixture. Bake as directed.

PESTO PINE NUT BISCUITS: Stir 3 tbsp. (50 mL) basil pesto into buttermilk. Add to flour mixture with 1/2 cup (125 mL) chopped, toasted pine nuts. Bake as directed.

SPICE DROP BISCUITS: Add 1/2 tsp. (2 mL) ground cinnamon and 1/4 tsp. (1 mL) ground allspice to flour mixture. Increase buttermilk to 1 cup (250 mL). Stir in 1/4 cup (60 mL) minced crystallized ginger when adding buttermilk to flour mixture. Drop by level 1/4 cup (60 mL) onto greased baking sheet. Combine 2 tbsp. (30 mL) granulated sugar and 1/8 tsp. (0.5 mL) ground cinnamon. Sprinkle on top. Bake as directed.

Sesame Cornbread Scones

Cornbread texture complemented by cheese, onion and
toasted sesame seeds. Satisfying with soup or stew.

All-purpose flour	1 1/2 cups	375 mL
Yellow cornmeal	1 cup	250 mL
Baking powder	4 tsp.	20 mL
Salt	1/2 tsp.	2 mL
Cold butter (or hard margarine), cut up	1/3 cup	75 mL
Large egg, fork-beaten	1	1
Grated sharp Cheddar cheese	3/4 cup	175 mL
Milk	2/3 cup	150 mL
Sliced green onion	1/4 cup	60 mL
Milk	2 tsp.	10 mL
Sesame seeds	1 tbsp.	15 mL

Combine first 4 ingredients in large bowl. Cut in butter until mixture resembles coarse crumbs. Make a well in centre.

Add next 4 ingredients to well. Stir until soft dough forms. Turn out onto lightly floured surface. Knead 6 times. Roll or pat out to 9 inch (22 cm) round. Transfer to greased baking sheet.

Brush with second amount of milk. Sprinkle with sesame seeds. Score 8 wedges in dough, about 1/2 inch (12 mm) deep, using sharp knife. Bake in centre of 375°F (190°C) oven for 20 to 25 minutes until wooden pick inserted in centre comes out clean and edges are golden. Let stand on baking sheet for 5 minutes before removing to wire rack. Cuts into 8 wedges.

1 wedge: 301 Calories; 13.8 g Total Fat (4.0 g Mono, 1.0 g Poly, 7.9 g Sat); 61 mg Cholesterol; 35 g Carbohydrate; 2 g Fibre; 9 g Protein; 507 mg Sodium

Pictured on front cover.

CHILI JACK SCONES: Add 1/2 tsp. (2 mL) chili powder to flour mixture. Use jalapeño Monterey Jack cheese instead of Cheddar cheese. Bake as directed.

Lemon Yogurt Triangles

Serve with fresh berries and whipped cream for a shortcake-style dessert.

All-purpose flour	1 1/2 cups	375 mL
Whole wheat flour	1/2 cup	125 mL
Granulated sugar	2 tbsp.	30 mL
Baking powder	1 tbsp.	15 mL
Baking soda	1/2 tsp.	2 mL
Salt	1/2 tsp.	2 mL
Grated lemon zest	1 1/2 tsp.	7 mL
Cold butter (or hard margarine), cut up	1/2 cup	125 mL
Vanilla (or plain) yogurt	1 cup	250 mL
GLAZE		
Lemon juice	1 1/2 tsp.	7 mL
Icing (confectioner's) sugar	1/4 cup	60 mL

Combine first 7 ingredients in large bowl. Cut in butter until mixture resembles coarse crumbs. Make a well in centre.

Add yogurt to well. Stir until soft dough forms. Turn out onto lightly floured surface. Gently knead 4 or 5 times until dough just comes together. Roll out to 6 x 9 inch (15 x 22 cm) rectangle. Transfer to greased baking sheet. Score 6 rectangles in dough, about 1/2 inch (12 mm) deep, using greased sharp knife. Score each rectangle into 2 triangles, for a total of 12 triangles (see diagram). Cut through dough at score marks, almost to bottom of pan. Bake in 400°F (205°C) oven for 18 to 20 minutes until golden. Let stand on baking sheet until cooled completely.

Glaze: Stir lemon juice into icing sugar in small bowl until smooth. Drizzle in zigzag pattern over cooled triangles. Cuts into 12 triangles.

1 triangle: 189 Calories; 8.8 g Total Fat (2.5 g Mono, 0.4 g Poly, 5.4 g Sat); 23 mg Cholesterol; 25 g Carbohydrate; 1 g Fibre; 3 g Protein; 341 mg Sodium

Pictured on page 125.

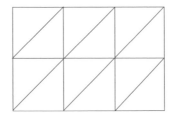

Chocolate Coconut Biscuits

A rich and fluffy drop biscuit. A dusting of icing sugar sweetens these up nicely!

All-purpose flour	2 cups	500 mL
Granulated sugar	1/3 cup	75 mL
Cocoa, sifted if lumpy	2 tbsp.	30 mL
Baking powder	2 tsp.	10 mL
Baking soda	1 tsp.	5 mL
Salt	1/2 tsp.	2 mL
Cold butter (or hard margarine), cut up	1/3 cup	75 mL
Milk	2/3 cup	150 mL
Medium unsweetened coconut	1/2 cup	125 mL
Sour cream	1/2 cup	125 mL
Coconut extract	1/2 tsp.	2 mL

Icing (confectioner's) sugar, for dusting

Combine first 6 ingredients in large bowl. Cut in butter until mixture resembles coarse crumbs. Make a well in centre.

Add next 4 ingredients to well. Stir until soft dough forms. Turn out onto lightly floured surface. Knead 8 times. Drop dough by level 1/4 cup (60 mL) about 1 inch (2.5 cm) apart onto greased baking sheet. Bake in 400°F (205°C) oven for 12 to 15 minutes until firm to the touch. Let stand on baking sheet for 5 minutes before removing to wire rack.

Dust with icing sugar. Makes about 12 biscuits.

1 biscuit: 200 Calories; 9.8 g Total Fat (2.2 g Mono, 0.4 g Poly, 6.7 g Sat); 19 mg Cholesterol; 25 g Carbohydrate; 1 g Fibre; 4 g Protein; 336 mg Sodium

Pictured on page 125.

Paré Pointer
When playing cards with pickles, they dill you in.

Savoury Stuffing Wedges

Traditional stuffing flavours baked into a scone-like cake. A perfect side dish to BBQ chicken, ribs or a bowl of potato cheese soup. Chill leftovers.

Bacon slices, diced	12	12
Chopped celery	1 cup	250 mL
Chopped onion	1 cup	250 mL
All-purpose flour	2 1/2 cups	625 mL
Yellow cornmeal	1/2 cup	125 mL
Baking powder	2 tbsp.	30 mL
Dried sage	1 tbsp.	15 mL
Parsley flakes	1 tbsp.	15 mL
Salt	1/2 tsp.	2 mL
Pepper	1/2 tsp.	2 mL
Cold butter (or hard margarine), cut up	1/2 cup	125 mL
Milk	1 cup	250 mL
Dijon-flavoured mayonnaise	2 tbsp.	30 mL

Cook bacon in large frying pan on medium until crisp. Transfer with slotted spoon to paper towels to drain.

Heat 1 tbsp. (15 mL) drippings in same pan on medium. Add celery and onion. Cook for 5 to 10 minutes, stirring often, until onion is softened. Transfer to medium bowl. Add bacon. Set aside.

Combine next 7 ingredients in large bowl. Cut in butter until mixture resembles coarse crumbs. Make a well in centre.

Add milk and mayonnaise to bacon mixture. Stir. Add to well. Stir until just moistened. Transfer to greased 9 inch (22 cm) deep dish pie plate. Gently press to edge of plate. Score 8 wedges in dough, about 1/2 inch (12 mm) deep, using sharp knife. Bake in 375°F (190°C) oven for about 40 minutes until wooden pick inserted in centre comes out clean. Let stand in pie plate for 10 minutes before removing to wire rack. Cuts into 8 wedges.

1 wedge: 388 Calories; 19.4 g Total Fat (6.8 g Mono, 1.8 g Poly, 9.7 g Sat); 43 mg Cholesterol; 44 g Carbohydrate; 2 g Fibre; 10 g Protein; 769 mg Sodium

Pictured on page 126.

Green Onion Biscuits

Mild green onion flavour makes these a tasty addition to soup or stew.
Also delicious on their own with a pat of butter on the side.

All-purpose flour	3 cups	750 mL
Baking powder	4 tsp.	20 mL
Salt	1 tsp.	5 mL
Dry mustard	1/2 tsp.	2 mL
Cold butter (or hard margarine), cut up	1/2 cup	125 mL
Milk	1 1/4 cups	300 mL
Sliced green onion	1/2 cup	125 mL
Chopped fresh parsley (or 1 tbsp., 15 mL, flakes)	1/4 cup	60 mL
Milk	1 tbsp.	15 mL
Paprika	1 1/2 tsp.	7 mL

Combine first 4 ingredients in large bowl. Cut in butter until mixture resembles coarse crumbs. Make a well in centre.

Add next 3 ingredients to well. Stir until soft dough forms. Turn out onto lightly floured surface. Knead 8 times. Roll or pat out to 3/4 inch (2 cm) thickness. Cut out circles with lightly floured 2 1/2 inch (6.4 cm) biscuit cutter. Arrange about 2 inches (5 cm) apart on greased baking sheet.

Brush tops with second amount of milk. Sprinkle with paprika. Bake in 425°F (220°C) oven for 15 to 20 minutes until golden. Let stand on baking sheet for 5 minutes before removing to wire rack to cool. Makes about 12 biscuits.

1 biscuit: 208 Calories; 8.8 g Total Fat (2.5 g Mono, 0.5 g Poly, 5.3 g Sat); 23 mg Cholesterol; 28 g Carbohydrate; 1 g Fibre; 5 g Protein; 420 mg Sodium

Pictured on page 126.

Pepper Lime Damper

Damper was a staple of bush settlers who lived in the outback of Australia. Serve with bean soup for a hearty meal.

All-purpose flour	3 1/2 cups	875 mL
Granulated sugar	1 tbsp.	15 mL
Baking powder	1 tbsp.	15 mL
Coarse ground pepper	2 tsp.	10 mL
Baking soda	1 tsp.	5 mL
Salt	1/2 tsp.	2 mL
Cold butter (or hard margarine), cut up	1/4 cup	60 mL
Buttermilk (or soured milk, see Tip, page 13)	3/4 cup	175 mL
Juice of 2 limes, plus water, to make	3/4 cup	175 mL
Finely grated lime zest	2 tbsp.	30 mL
Buttermilk (or soured milk, see Tip, page 13)	2 tsp.	10 mL

Combine first 6 ingredients in large bowl. Cut in butter until mixture resembles coarse crumbs. Make a well in centre.

Add next 3 ingredients to well. Stir until soft dough forms. Turn out onto lightly floured surface. Knead 8 times. Roll or pat out to 8 inch (20 cm) round on greased baking sheet. Cut "+" on top of dough, about 1/2 inch (12 mm) deep and 5 inches (12.5 cm) across, using sharp knife.

Brush with second amount of buttermilk. Bake in 375°F (190°C) oven for 30 to 35 minutes until wooden pick inserted in centre comes out clean. Let stand on baking sheet for 5 minutes before removing to wire rack. Cuts into 8 wedges.

1 wedge: 286 Calories; 7.0 g Total Fat (1.9 g Mono, 0.5 g Poly, 4.1 g Sat); 17 mg Cholesterol; 49 g Carbohydrate; 2 g Fibre; 7 g Protein; 539 mg Sodium

Biscuits & Scones

Figgy Orange Scones

Sweet, chewy fig bites in an orange-flavoured scone. Great for afternoon tea with butter or marmalade. Lighter texture than most other scones, therefore no need to score before baking.

All-purpose flour	3/4 cup	175 mL
Whole wheat flour	1/2 cup	125 mL
Baking powder	2 tsp.	10 mL
Salt	1/8 tsp.	0.5 mL
Cold butter (or hard margarine), cut up	2 tbsp.	30 mL
Chopped dried figs	1/2 cup	125 mL
Granulated sugar	1/4 cup	60 mL
Grated orange zest	1 tsp.	5 mL
Buttermilk (or soured milk, see Tip, page 13)	2/3 cup	150 mL
Large egg, fork-beaten	1	1
Granulated sugar	1 tsp.	5 mL

Combine first 4 ingredients in large bowl. Cut in butter until mixture resembles coarse crumbs.

Add next 3 ingredients. Stir. Make a well in centre.

Add buttermilk and egg to well. Stir until just moistened. Spread in greased 8 inch (20 cm) round pan.

Sprinkle with second amount of sugar. Bake in 375°F (190°C) oven for about 25 minutes until golden. Let stand in pan for 5 minutes before removing to wire rack. Cuts into 8 wedges.

1 wedge: 178 Calories; 4.2 g Total Fat (1.2 g Mono, 0.4 g Poly, 2.2 g Sat); 36 mg Cholesterol; 32 g Carbohydrate; 3 g Fibre; 4 g Protein; 194 mg Sodium

Paré Pointer
Stolen candy is better known as hot chocolate.

From pull-aparts to coffee cakes, this section boasts quick breads with a twist. It might be something simple like an interesting icing or streusel topping, or it may be a who-would-have-guessed-it shape, such as our whole wheat pizza crust. Guests will think you took hours to make one of the following recipes, but you'll know that these specialty breads were...quick! Please glance through Tips for Terrific Quick Breads on page 8.

Blueberry Cream Braid

A decorative, pastry-like braid suitable for special occasions.
Make it with fresh blueberries—never frozen—for optimum flavour.

All-purpose flour	2 cups	500 mL
Granulated sugar	1/4 cup	60 mL
Baking powder	2 tsp.	10 mL
Salt	1/2 tsp.	2 mL
Cold butter (or hard margarine), cut up	1/4 cup	60 mL
Sour cream	1/3 cup	75 mL
Milk	1/3 cup	75 mL
Vanilla extract	1 tsp.	5 mL
Egg yolk (large)	1	1
Blueberry spreadable cream cheese	1/2 cup	125 mL
Granulated sugar	1/4 cup	60 mL
Grated lemon zest	2 tsp.	10 mL
Vanilla extract	1 tsp.	5 mL
Fresh blueberries	1 cup	250 mL
Egg white (large)	1	1
Water	1 tbsp.	15 mL
GLAZE		
Lemon juice	1 tbsp.	15 mL
Icing (confectioner's) sugar	1/2 cup	125 mL

(continued on next page)

Measure first 4 ingredients into large bowl. Stir. Cut in butter until mixture resembles coarse crumbs. Make a well in centre.

Combine next 3 ingredients in small bowl until smooth. Add to well. Stir until soft dough forms. Turn out onto lightly floured surface. Knead gently 10 times. Roll or pat out to 12 × 15 inch (30 × 38 cm) rectangle on large ungreased baking sheet.

Beat next 5 ingredients in separate small bowl until smooth. Spread in 4 inch (10 cm) wide strip down centre of dough, leaving 1 inch (2.5 cm) space on both ends.

Sprinkle blueberries over cream cheese mixture. Cut dough at an angle into 1 inch (2.5 cm) strips, starting 1 inch (2.5 cm) away from sides of filling out to edge (see diagram). Discard irregular pieces. Fold top and bottom edges over filling. Starting at top, cross alternating strips from each side over filling, allowing strips to overlap in middle.

Beat egg white and water in small cup until frothy. Brush over crossed strips. Bake on centre rack in 425°F (220°C) oven for about 20 minutes until golden and firm to the touch. Let stand on baking sheet for 15 minutes.

Glaze: Stir lemon juice into icing sugar in small cup until smooth. Drizzle over warm braid. Cuts into 12 slices.

1 slice: 224 Calories; 7.8 g Total Fat (2.3 g Mono, 0.4 g Poly, 4.5 g Sat); 38 mg Cholesterol; 34 g Carbohydrate; 1 g Fibre; 4 g Protein; 287 mg Sodium

Pictured on page 35.

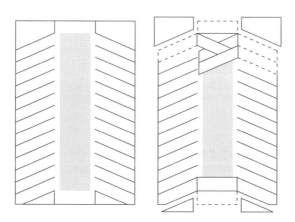

Quick Wheat Pizza Crust

*Convenient quick bread crust for the times you need pizza
in a hurry! Use your favourite toppings, bake and enjoy!*

All-purpose flour	1 1/4 cups	300 mL
Whole wheat flour	3/4 cup	175 mL
Granulated sugar	2 tsp.	10 mL
Baking powder	2 tsp.	10 mL
Baking soda	1 tsp.	5 mL
Salt	1/2 tsp.	2 mL
Buttermilk (or soured milk, see Tip, page 13)	2/3 cup	150 mL
Cooking oil	3 tbsp.	50 mL
Fancy (mild) molasses	1 tbsp.	15 mL

Measure first 6 ingredients into large bowl. Stir. Make a well in centre.

Add remaining 3 ingredients to well. Stir until soft dough forms. Turn out onto lightly floured surface. Knead 8 times. Press into greased 12 inch (30 cm) pizza pan. Top with your favourite sauce and toppings. Bake in 425°F (220°C) oven for about 10 minutes until crust is golden. Cuts into 8 wedges.

*1 wedge (crust only): 182 Calories; 5.8 g Total Fat (3.2 g Mono, 1.7 g Poly, 0.6 g Sat);
1 mg Cholesterol; 29 g Carbohydrate; 2 g Fibre; 4 g Protein; 426 mg Sodium*

1. Chocolate Coconut Biscuits, page 117
2. Lemon Yogurt Triangles, page 116
3. Basic Buttermilk Biscuits, page 114

Props courtesy of: Anchor Hocking Canada
Cherison Enterprises Inc.

Pistachio Lime Teacakes

Very rich and buttery—delicious! Dust with icing sugar for a pretty presentation.

Butter	3/4 cup	175 mL
Egg whites (large)	6	6
Icing (confectioner's) sugar	2 cups	500 mL
Ground almonds	3/4 cup	175 mL
Pistachios, toasted (see Tip, page 95) and chopped	2/3 cup	150 mL
All-purpose flour	1/2 cup	125 mL
Finely grated lime zest	2 tsp.	10 mL

Melt butter in small saucepan. Remove from heat. Cool slightly.

Beat egg whites in large bowl until frothy.

Add remaining 5 ingredients. Stir until just combined. Add butter. Stir. Fill greased muffin cups 3/4 full. Bake in 375°F (190°C) oven for about 20 minutes until wooden pick inserted in centre of muffin comes out clean. Let stand in pan for 5 minutes before removing to wire rack. Makes 12 teacakes.

1 teacake: 290 Calories; 18.5 g Total Fat (7.7 g Mono, 1.5 g Poly, 8.3 g Sat); 33 mg Cholesterol; 29 g Carbohydrate; 1 g Fibre; 4 g Protein; 152 mg Sodium

1. Roasted Pepper Ring, 130
2. Green Onion Biscuits, page 119
3. Spinach Cheese Pinwheels, page 128
4. Savoury Stuffing Wedges, page 118

Props courtesy of: Casa Bugatti
Totally Bamboo
Cherison Enterprises Inc.

Spinach Cheese Pinwheels

Spiral biscuits that taste as good as they look!
Fantastic with a bowl of tomato soup.

Box of frozen spinach, thawed, squeezed dry, finely chopped	10 oz.	300 g
Ricotta cheese	1/2 cup	125 mL
Grated sharp Cheddar cheese	1/2 cup	125 mL
Basil pesto	1/4 cup	60 mL
All-purpose flour	3 cups	750 mL
Baking powder	1 tbsp.	15 mL
Salt	1/2 tsp.	2 mL
Cold butter (or hard margarine), cut up	1/2 cup	125 mL
Milk	1 cup	250 mL
Butter (or hard margarine), melted	2 tbsp.	30 mL
Grated sharp Cheddar cheese	1/2 cup	125 mL

Combine first 4 ingredients in small bowl. Set aside.

Measure next 3 ingredients into large bowl. Stir. Cut in first amount of butter until mixture resembles coarse crumbs. Make a well in centre.

Add milk. Stir until soft dough forms. Turn out onto lightly floured surface. Knead 8 times. Roll or pat out to 10 × 12 inch (25 × 30 cm) rectangle. Spread spinach mixture on dough, leaving 1 inch (2.5 cm) edge on 1 long side. Roll up from long covered side, jelly roll-style. Pinch seam against roll to seal. Cut into 12 slices. Lay slices flat, about 1 inch (2.5 cm) apart on greased baking sheet.

Brush with second amount of butter. Sprinkle with second amount of cheese. Bake in 400°F (205°C) oven for about 20 minutes until golden. Let stand on baking sheet for 5 minutes before removing to wire rack. Makes 12 pinwheels.

1 pinwheel: 296 Calories; 16.9 g Total Fat (5.5 g Mono, 0.8 g Poly, 9.7 g Sat); 44 mg Cholesterol; 28 g Carbohydrate; 2 g Fibre; 9 g Protein; 392 mg Sodium

Pictured on page 126.

Pumpkin Snack Cake

Easy-to-hold wedges make this a perfect
not-too-sweet snack for kids! Comfort food.

All-purpose flour	1 1/4 cups	300 mL
Whole wheat flour	1 cup	250 mL
Brown sugar, packed	1/2 cup	125 mL
Baking powder	1 1/2 tsp.	7 mL
Baking soda	1/2 tsp.	2 mL
Ground cinnamon	1/2 tsp.	2 mL
Ground nutmeg	1/4 tsp.	1 mL
Ground ginger	1/4 tsp.	1 mL
Salt	1/4 tsp.	1 mL
Cold butter (or hard margarine), cut up	6 tbsp.	100 mL
Buttermilk (or soured milk, see Tip, page 13)	1 cup	250 mL
Canned pure pumpkin (no spices), (see Tip, page 83)	3/4 cup	175 mL
Chopped walnuts (optional)	1/2 cup	125 mL
Milk	1 tbsp.	15 mL
Brown sugar, packed	1 tbsp.	15 mL

Measure first 9 ingredients into large bowl. Stir. Cut in butter until mixture resembles coarse crumbs. Make a well in centre.

Combine next 3 ingredients in small bowl. Add to well. Stir until just moistened. Spread in greased 9 inch (22 cm) round baking pan.

Brush with milk. Sprinkle with second amount of brown sugar. Bake in 400°F (205°C) oven for about 30 minutes until wooden pick inserted in centre comes out clean. Let stand in pan for 10 minutes before removing to wire rack. Cuts into 8 wedges.

1 wedge: 291 Calories; 9.7 g Total Fat (2.7 g Mono, 0.6 g Poly, 5.8 g Sat); 25 mg Cholesterol; 47 g Carbohydrate; 3 g Fibre; 6 g Protein; 357 mg Sodium

Roasted Pepper Ring

*Golden biscuit ring with a crisp, orange cheese top and
roasted red pepper and herb flavour throughout.*

All-purpose flour	3 cups	750 mL
Baking powder	2 tbsp.	30 mL
Dried oregano	1/2 tsp.	2 mL
Paprika	1/2 tsp.	2 mL
Salt	1/2 tsp.	2 mL
Pepper	1/4 tsp.	1 mL
Garlic powder	1/4 tsp.	1 mL
Cold butter (or hard margarine)	1/2 cup	125 mL
Buttermilk (or soured milk, see Tip, page 13)	1 cup	250 mL
Roasted red peppers, drained and blotted dry, finely chopped	1/2 cup	125 mL
Butter (or hard margarine), melted	2 tbsp.	30 mL
Garlic powder	1/2 tsp.	2 mL
Paprika	1/4 tsp.	1 mL
Grated sharp Cheddar cheese	1/4 cup	60 mL

Measure first 7 ingredients into large bowl. Stir. Cut in first amount of
butter until mixture resembles coarse crumbs. Make a well in centre.

Add buttermilk and red pepper. Stir until soft dough forms. Turn out
onto lightly floured surface. Knead 8 times. Roll or pat out to 3/4 inch
(2 cm) thickness. Cut out circles with lightly floured 2 1/2 inch (6.4 cm)
biscuit cutter.

Combine next 3 ingredients in small bowl. Brush tops with 1/2 of butter
mixture. Arrange circles, standing on sides with inner edges touching to
keep upright, in circular pattern in greased 9 inch (22 cm) pie plate. Bake
in 375°F (190°C) oven for 20 minutes.

Sprinkle with cheese. Bake for another 20 minutes until cheese is golden
and wooden pick inserted in ring comes out clean. Brush with remaining
1/2 of butter mixture. Let stand for 5 minutes. Cuts into 12 wedges.

*1 wedge: 232 Calories; 11.4 g Total Fat (3.2 g Mono, 0.6 g Poly, 6.7 g Sat); 31 mg Cholesterol;
28 g Carbohydrate; 1 g Fibre; 5 g Protein; 426 mg Sodium*

Pictured on page 126.

Maple Gingerbread

Warm, comforting spices and bites of ginger baked into moist gingerbread. Drizzled with sweet maple glaze—yum!

All-purpose flour	1 1/2 cups	375 mL
Ground ginger	2 tsp.	10 mL
Baking soda	1 tsp.	5 mL
Ground cinnamon	1 tsp.	5 mL
Salt	1/2 tsp.	2 mL
Ground cloves	1/4 tsp.	1 mL
Minced crystallized ginger	1/2 cup	125 mL
Fancy (mild) molasses	1/3 cup	75 mL
Maple (or maple-flavoured) syrup	1/4 cup	60 mL
Boiling water	3/4 cup	175 mL
Butter (or hard margarine), softened	1/4 cup	60 mL
Brown sugar, packed	1/4 cup	60 mL
Large egg	1	1
GLAZE		
Maple (or maple-flavoured) syrup	2 tbsp.	30 mL
Icing (confectioner's) sugar	1/4 cup	60 mL

Measure first 6 ingredients into small bowl. Stir. Set aside.

Combine next 3 ingredients in small heatproof bowl. Add boiling water. Stir until combined. Let stand for 5 minutes to cool.

Cream butter and brown sugar in large bowl. Add egg. Beat well. Add flour mixture in 3 parts alternating with molasses mixture in 2 parts, stirring after each addition until just combined. Spread in greased 9 x 9 inch (22 x 22 cm) baking pan. Bake in 350°F (175°C) oven for about 30 minutes until wooden pick inserted in centre comes out clean. Let stand for 10 minutes.

Glaze: Stir syrup into icing sugar in small bowl until smooth. Spread over warm gingerbread. Cuts into 16 pieces.

1 piece: 152 Calories; 3.6 g Total Fat (1.0 g Mono, 0.2 g Poly, 2.0 g Sat); 22 mg Cholesterol; 29 g Carbohydrate; 1 g Fibre; 2 g Protein; 197 mg Sodium

Fruited Muffin Bars

Instead of a muffin pan, these are baked in a square baking pan and cut into bars. Ideal for tea time and breakfast-on-the-go!

Boiling water	1 cup	250 mL
Orange pekoe tea bag	1	1
Chopped pitted dates	3/4 cup	175 mL
Dark raisins	1 cup	250 mL
Chopped dried cherries	1/4 cup	60 mL
Large egg, fork-beaten	1	1
Butter (or hard margarine), melted	1/4 cup	60 mL
All-purpose flour	2 cups	500 mL
Brown sugar, packed	3/4 cup	175 mL
Baking powder	1 tsp.	5 mL
Baking soda	1/2 tsp.	2 mL
Ground allspice	1/2 tsp.	2 mL
Ground ginger	1/2 tsp.	2 mL
Salt	1/2 tsp.	2 mL

Pour boiling water over tea bag in small heatproof bowl. Add next 3 ingredients. Let stand for 10 minutes. Squeeze and discard tea bag.

Add egg and butter. Stir.

Measure remaining 7 ingredients into large bowl. Stir. Make a well in centre. Add fruit mixture. Stir just until combined. Spread in greased 9 x 9 inch (22 x 22 cm) baking pan. Bake in 350°F (175°C) oven for about 30 minutes until wooden pick inserted in centre comes out clean. Let stand in pan for 10 minutes before removing to wire rack to cool. Cuts into 12 bars.

1 bar: 258 Calories; 5.0 g Total Fat (1.4 g Mono, 0.4 g Poly, 2.8 g Sat); 29 mg Cholesterol; 52 g Carbohydrate; 2 g Fibre; 4 g Protein; 239 mg Sodium

Pictured on page 18.

Marmalade Ginger Crowns

*Creamy ginger-orange custard filling sitting
in a pointed crown. Best served warm.*

All-purpose flour	2 cups	500 mL
Minced crystallized ginger	3 tbsp.	50 mL
Granulated sugar	2 tbsp.	30 mL
Baking powder	1 tbsp.	15 mL
Salt	1/2 tsp.	2 mL
Baking soda	1/4 tsp.	1 mL
Cold butter (or hard margarine), cut up	1/3 cup	75 mL
Large egg	1	1
Sour cream	1/2 cup	125 mL
Vanilla extract	1/2 tsp.	2 mL
Block of cream cheese, softened	4 oz.	125 g
Orange marmalade	1/4 cup	60 mL
Minced crystallized ginger	1 tbsp.	15 mL

Measure first 6 ingredients into medium bowl. Stir. Cut in butter until
mixture resembles coarse crumbs. Make a well in centre.

Combine next 3 ingredients in small bowl. Add to well. Stir until soft
dough forms. Turn out onto lightly floured surface. Knead 8 times. Roll
or pat out to 9 x 12 inch (22 x 30 cm) rectangle. Cut into twelve 3 inch
(7.5 cm) squares. Press into bottom and sides of 12 greased muffin cups.

Combine remaining 3 ingredients in separate small bowl. Spoon about
1 tbsp. (15 mL) mixture in each lined muffin cup. Bake in 425°F (220°C)
oven for about 15 minutes until pastry is golden. Let stand in pan for
10 minutes before removing to wire rack. Makes 12 crowns.

*1 crown: 221 Calories; 11.1 g Total Fat (3.2 g Mono, 0.5 g Poly, 6.7 g Sat); 48 mg Cholesterol;
27 g Carbohydrate; 1 g Fibre; 4 g Protein; 319 mg Sodium*

Pictured on page 143.

Caramel Nut Pull-Aparts

Sweet, satisfying caramel sauce smothers apple and nut pieces in tender biscuit pastry. This will be a hit for brunch or coffee hour. For a special presentation, use a decorative pie plate.

Tart medium cooking apples (such as Granny Smith), peeled and chopped	2	2
Water	3 tbsp.	50 mL
Granulated sugar	1 tbsp.	15 mL
All-purpose flour	2 cups	500 mL
Baking powder	1 tbsp.	15 mL
Salt	1/4 tsp.	1 mL
Cold butter (or hard margarine), cut up	1/4 cup	60 mL
Milk	3/4 cup	175 mL
Butter (or hard margarine), melted	1 tbsp.	15 mL
Brown sugar, packed	1/3 cup	75 mL
Walnut pieces, toasted (see Tip, page 95) and chopped	1/4 cup	60 mL
Ground cinnamon	1/2 tsp.	2 mL
CARAMEL SAUCE		
Whipping cream	1/4 cup	60 mL
Butter (or hard margarine)	1/4 cup	60 mL
Brown sugar, packed	1/4 cup	60 mL
Large marshmallows, quartered	4	4
Walnut pieces, toasted (see Tip, page 95) and finely chopped	1 tbsp.	15 mL

Combine first 3 ingredients in small saucepan. Cover. Cook on medium for about 10 minutes, stirring occasionally, until apple is tender. Drain well. Cool.

Measure next 3 ingredients into large bowl. Stir. Cut in first amount of butter until mixture resembles coarse crumbs. Make a well in centre.

Add milk to well. Stir until soft dough forms. Turn out onto lightly floured surface. Knead 8 times. Roll out to 8 x 16 inch (20 x 40 cm) rectangle.

(continued on next page)

Brush with second amount of butter, leaving 1 inch (2.5 cm) edge on both long sides.

Combine next 3 ingredients in small bowl. Add apple. Stir. Sprinkle over dough. Roll up from 1 long side, jelly-roll style. Pinch seam against roll to seal. Cut into 12 slices. Arrange slices, standing upright with cut sides together, in circular pattern, in greased 9 inch (22 cm) round pan or deep dish pie plate. Bake on centre rack in 400°F (205°C) oven for about 25 minutes until golden. Let stand for 5 minutes.

Caramel Sauce: Combine all 4 ingredients in medium saucepan. Heat and stir on medium until marshmallows are melted and brown sugar is dissolved. Cool slightly. Makes about 1/2 cup (125 mL) sauce. Drizzle over warm pull-aparts.

Sprinkle with second amount of walnuts. Makes 12 pull-aparts.

1 pull-apart: 272 Calories; 13.3 g Total Fat (3.7 g Mono, 1.8 g Poly, 7.0 g Sat); 31 mg Cholesterol; 36 g Carbohydrate; 1 g Fibre; 4 g Protein; 251 mg Sodium

Pictured on page 143.

Paré Pointer
The invisible man will only drink evaporated milk.

Old-Fashioned Coffee Cake

Rich crumble topping covers a layer of fruit on moist, sweet cake.
Try it with your favourite flavour of pie filling. Delicious served
with vanilla ice cream or a dollop of whipped cream.

All-purpose flour	2 cups	500 mL
Granulated sugar	1 cup	250 mL
Baking powder	2 tsp.	10 mL
Salt	1/4 tsp.	1 mL
Cold butter (or hard margarine), cut up	1/2 cup	125 mL
Large egg, fork-beaten	1	1
Milk	3/4 cup	175 mL
Can of cherry pie filling	19 oz.	540 mL
TOPPING		
Brown sugar, packed	1 cup	250 mL
All-purpose flour	1 cup	250 mL
Cold butter (or hard margarine), cut up	1/2 cup	125 mL

Measure first 4 ingredients into large bowl. Stir. Cut in butter until mixture resembles coarse crumbs. Make a well in centre.

Add egg and milk to well. Stir until just moistened. Spread in greased 9 x 13 inch (22 x 33 cm) baking pan.

Carefully spread pie filling on top.

Topping: Combine brown sugar and flour in small bowl. Cut butter until mixture resembles coarse crumbs. Sprinkle over pie filling. Bake in 375°F (190°C) oven for about 40 minutes until top is golden and filling bubbles at edges. Let stand for 10 minutes. Cuts into 15 pieces.

1 piece: 380 Calories; 13.8 g Total Fat (4.0 g Mono, 0.7 g Poly, 8.3 g Sat); 50 mg Cholesterol; 62 g Carbohydrate; 1 g Fibre; 4 g Protein; 242 mg Sodium

Pictured on page 143.

Creamy Carrot Coffee Cake

*Creamy decadence atop nutty carrot cake. A special treat
for morning coffee or fancy enough for a birthday cake!*

All-purpose flour	2 cups	500 mL
Granulated sugar	1 1/2 cups	375 mL
Ground cinnamon	2 tsp.	10 mL
Baking powder	1 1/2 tsp.	7 mL
Baking soda	1 tsp.	5 mL
Salt	1/2 tsp.	2 mL
Large eggs	3	3
Cooking oil	2/3 cup	150 mL
Vanilla extract	2 tsp.	10 mL
Grated carrot	1 1/3 cups	325 mL
Drained canned crushed pineapple, juice reserved	1/2 cup	125 mL
Chopped walnuts	1 cup	250 mL
ICING		
Icing (confectioner's) sugar	1 cup	250 mL
Block of cream cheese, softened	4 oz.	125 g
Butter (or hard margarine), softened	1/4 cup	60 mL
Reserved pineapple juice	2 – 3 tbsp.	30 – 50 mL

Measure first 6 ingredients into large bowl. Stir. Make a well in centre.

Beat next 3 ingredients with whisk in medium bowl. Add carrot, pineapple
and walnuts. Stir. Add to well. Stir until just moistened. Spread in greased
12 cup (3 L) bundt pan. Bake in 350°F (175°C) oven for about 50 minutes
until wooden pick inserted in centre of cake comes out clean. Let stand
in pan for 10 minutes before removing to wire rack to cool. Place on
serving plate.

Icing: Beat icing sugar, cream cheese and butter in small bowl until
smooth. Gradually add pineapple juice until barely pourable consistency.
Spoon over cake, allowing to drizzle down sides. Cuts into 16 wedges.

*1 wedge: 383 Calories; 21.2 g Total Fat (8.7 g Mono, 6.4 g Poly, 4.9 g Sat); 57 mg Cholesterol;
44 g Carbohydrate; 1 g Fibre; 6 g Protein; 259 mg Sodium*

Allergy-Sensitive Muffins

Muffins are such a friendly, homey treat, easily shared with everyone. To make sure no one is left out, we've developed 11 recipes for those who are sensitive to certain types of food, whether it's eggs, sugar, dairy, wheat or gluten. These muffins are so tasty, you'll soon add them to your favourites. Some points to consider:

- Gluten-free flours are often finely powdered. Mix them well with other dry ingredients before adding the wet mixture.

- It is the gluten that causes muffins to round. Don't be surprised if your gluten-free muffins are flatter or slightly smaller than regular muffins.

- To make 1 tbsp. (15 mL) gluten-free baking powder, combine 1 tsp. (5 mL) baking soda with 2 tsp. (10 mL) cream of tartar.

Breakfast Muesli Muffins

No added fat or egg. For best results, do not use non-fat yogurt.

All-purpose flour	1 1/2 cups	375 mL
Baking powder	2 tsp.	10 mL
Baking soda	1/2 tsp.	2 mL
Salt	1/2 tsp.	2 mL
Ground ginger	1/2 tsp.	2 mL
Cooked oatmeal (see Note)	1 cup	250 mL
Liquid honey	1/2 cup	125 mL
Plain yogurt	1/2 cup	125 mL
Golden raisins	1/2 cup	125 mL
Chopped walnuts	1/2 cup	125 mL
Finely chopped dried apricot	1/4 cup	60 mL

Measure first 5 ingredients into large bowl. Stir. Make a well in centre.

Beat next 3 ingredients with whisk in medium bowl. Add to well.

Add remaining 3 ingredients. Stir until just moistened. Fill 12 greased muffin cups 3/4 full. Bake in 375°F (190°C) oven for 18 to 20 minutes until wooden pick inserted in centre of muffin comes out clean. Let stand in pan for 5 minutes before removing to wire rack to cool. Makes 12 muffins.

(continued on next page)

1 muffin: 197 Calories; 3.8 g Total Fat (0.9 g Mono, 2.3 g Poly, 0.4 g Sat); 1 mg Cholesterol; 39 g Carbohydrate; 2 g Fibre; 5 g Protein; 250 mg Sodium

Pictured on page 18.

Note: To make 1 cup (250 mL) cooked oatmeal, combine 1/2 cup (125 mL) quick-cooking rolled oats, 1/8 tsp. (0.5 mL) salt and 1 cup (250 mL) water in small saucepan. Bring to a boil on medium. Boil gently for about 5 minutes, stirring constantly, until thickened. Cool completely before using in muffins.

No-Egg Chocolate Muffins

Perfectly balanced orange and chocolate flavours in a moist, snacking muffin.

All-purpose flour	1 cup	250 mL
Whole wheat flour	1 cup	250 mL
Granulated sugar	2/3 cup	150 mL
Cocoa powder, sifted if lumpy	1/4 cup	60 mL
Baking powder	2 tsp.	10 mL
Baking soda	1 tsp.	5 mL
Salt	1/4 tsp.	1 mL
Orange juice	1/2 cup	125 mL
Water	1/3 cup	75 mL
Cooking oil	1/3 cup	75 mL
White vinegar	1 tbsp.	15 mL
Grated orange peel	1 tbsp.	15 mL
Vanilla extract	1 tsp.	5 mL
Mini semi-sweet chocolate chips	1 cup	250 mL

Measure first 7 ingredients into large bowl. Stir. Make a well in centre.

Combine next 6 ingredients in medium bowl. Add to well.

Add chocolate chips. Stir until just moistened. Fill 12 greased muffin cups 2/3 full. Bake in 375°F (190°C) oven for 18 to 20 minutes until wooden pick inserted in centre of muffin comes out clean. Let stand in pan for 5 minutes before removing to wire rack to cool. Makes 12 muffins.

1 muffin: 260 Calories; 11.4 g Total Fat (5.4 g Mono, 2.2 g Poly, 3.3 g Sat); 0 mg Cholesterol; 40 g Carbohydrate; 3 g Fibre; 4 g Protein; 221 mg Sodium

Pictured on page 144.

Cherry Coconut Muffins

Perfect for your lactose-intolerant or dairy-sensitive guests.

All-purpose flour	3 cups	750 mL
Granulated sugar	1 cup	250 mL
Medium unsweetened coconut	1 cup	250 mL
Baking powder	1 tbsp.	15 mL
Salt	1/2 tsp.	2 mL
Large egg	1	1
Can of light coconut milk	14 oz.	398 mL
Grated lemon zest	1 tbsp.	15 mL
Pitted sour cherries, well drained, blotted dry and chopped	1 cup	250 mL

Measure first 5 ingredients into large bowl. Stir. Make a well in centre.

Combine next 3 ingredients in medium bowl. Add to well.

Add cherries. Stir until just moistened. Fill 12 greased muffin cups full. Bake in 375°F (190°C) oven for about 25 minutes until wooden pick inserted in centre of muffin comes out clean and tops are golden. Let stand in pan for 5 minutes before removing to wire rack to cool. Makes 12 muffins.

1 muffin: 287 Calories; 8.8 g Total Fat (0.4 g Mono, 0.3 g Poly, 7.3 g Sat); 18 mg Cholesterol; 48 g Carbohydrate; 2 g Fibre; 5 g Protein; 206 mg Sodium

Pictured on page 144.

Eggless Pumpkin Muffins

Lightly spiced, dense pumpkin muffins—with no egg!

All-purpose flour	2 1/2 cups	625 mL
Brown sugar, packed	1 cup	250 mL
Baking soda	1 tbsp.	15 mL
Ground coriander	1/2 tsp.	2 mL
Ground cinnamon	1/2 tsp.	2 mL
Salt	1/2 tsp.	2 mL
Ground cloves	1/4 tsp.	1 mL

(continued on next page)

Can of pure pumpkin (no spices)	14 oz.	398 mL
Milk	1 cup	250 mL
Plain yogurt	1/2 cup	125 mL
Cooking oil	1/4 cup	60 mL

Measure first 7 ingredients into large bowl. Stir. Make a well in centre.

Combine remaining 4 ingredients in medium bowl. Add to well. Stir until just moistened. Fill 12 greased muffin cups full. Bake in 375°F (190°C) oven for about 25 minutes until wooden pick inserted in centre of muffin comes out clean. Let stand in pan for 5 minutes before removing to wire rack to cool. Makes 12 muffins.

1 muffin: 244 Calories; 5.6 g Total Fat (3.0 g Mono, 1.6 g Poly, 0.7 g Sat); 2 mg Cholesterol; 45 g Carbohydrate; 2 g Fibre; 5 g Protein; 448 mg Sodium

Low-Fat Chocolate Muffins

Curb your chocolate craving with these low-fat and egg-free muffins. Very satisfying.

All-purpose flour	1 3/4 cups	425 mL
Granulated sugar	2/3 cup	150 mL
Cocoa, sifted if lumpy	1/3 cup	75 mL
Natural wheat bran	1/4 cup	60 mL
Baking powder	2 tsp.	10 mL
Baking soda	1 tsp.	5 mL
Salt	1/2 tsp.	2 mL
Non-fat vanilla yogurt	3/4 cup	175 mL
Skim milk	3/4 cup	175 mL
Vanilla extract	1 tsp.	5 mL

Measure first 7 ingredients into large bowl. Stir. Make a well in centre.

Combine remaining 3 ingredients in medium bowl. Add to well. Stir until just moistened. Fill 12 greased muffin cups 3/4 full. Bake in 375°F (190°C) oven for 18 to 20 minutes until wooden pick inserted in centre of muffin comes out clean. Let stand in pan for 5 minutes before removing to wire rack to cool. Makes 12 muffins.

1 muffin: 139 Calories; 0.6 g Total Fat (0.2 g Mono, 0.1 g Poly, 0.3 g Sat); 1 mg Cholesterol; 31 g Carbohydrate; 2 g Fibre; 4 g Protein; 289 mg Sodium

Gluten-Free Chai Muffins

Wonderfully moist, fine-textured muffins filled with delicious, aromatic spices.

White (or brown) rice flour	1 1/2 cups	375 mL
Soy flour	1/2 cup	125 mL
Gluten-free baking powder (see Tip, page 147)	1 tsp.	5 mL
Baking soda	1 tsp.	5 mL
Ground cinnamon	1 tsp.	5 mL
Salt	1/2 tsp.	2 mL
Ground allspice	1/4 tsp.	1 mL
Ground nutmeg	1/4 tsp.	1 mL
Ground cardamom (optional)	1/4 tsp.	1 mL
Large eggs	2	2
Chai tea concentrate	3/4 cup	175 mL
Liquid honey	1/2 cup	125 mL
Cooking oil	1/4 cup	60 mL
Unsweetened applesauce	1/4 cup	60 mL
Vanilla yogurt	1/4 cup	60 mL

Measure first 9 ingredients into large bowl. Stir. Make a well in centre.

Combine remaining 6 ingredients in medium bowl. Add to well. Stir until just moistened. Batter will be thin. Fill 12 greased muffin cups 3/4 full. Bake in 375°F (190°C) oven for about 20 minutes until wooden pick inserted in centre of muffin comes out clean. Let stand in pan for 5 minutes before removing to wire rack to cool. Makes 12 muffins.

1 muffin: 215 Calories; 6.9 g Total Fat (3.5 g Mono, 2.1 g Poly, 0.9 g Sat); 36 mg Cholesterol; 36 g Carbohydrate; 1 g Fibre; 4 g Protein; 252 mg Sodium

1. Caramel Nut Pull-Aparts, page 134
2. Marmalade Ginger Crowns, page 133
3. Old-Fashioned Coffee Cake, page 136

Props courtesy of: Casa Bugatti
Cherison Enterprises Inc.
Pyrex®

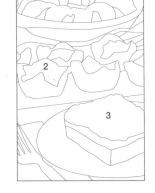

Almond Pear Muffins

Sugar-free. Crunchy nuts and tender pears in moist, chunky muffins.

All-purpose flour	2 1/2 cups	625 mL
Low-calorie sweetener (Splenda)	1/2 cup	125 mL
Baking powder	1 tbsp.	15 mL
Salt	1/4 tsp.	1 mL
Large eggs	2	2
Reserved pear juice	3/4 cup	175 mL
Milk	2/3 cup	150 mL
Cooking oil	1/4 cup	60 mL
Almond extract	1/2 tsp.	2 mL
Can of pear halves in juice, drained and juice reserved, chopped	14 oz.	398 mL
Whole almonds, toasted (see Tip, page 95) and chopped	1/2 cup	125 mL

Measure first 4 ingredients into large bowl. Stir. Make a well in centre.

Combine next 5 ingredients in medium bowl. Add to well.

Add pear and almonds. Stir until just moistened. Fill 12 greased muffin cups 3/4 full. Bake in 375°F (190°C) oven for 20 to 22 minutes until wooden pick inserted in centre of muffin comes out clean. Let stand in pan for 5 minutes before removing to wire rack to cool. Makes 12 muffins.

1 muffin: 216 Calories; 9.4 g Total Fat (5.4 g Mono, 2.4 g Poly, 1.1 g Sat); 36 mg Cholesterol; 28 g Carbohydrate; 2 g Fibre; 6 g Protein; 162 mg Sodium

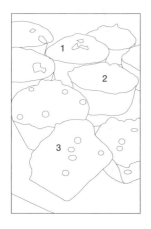

1. Cherry Coconut Muffins, page 140
2. "Free" Muffins, page 149
3. No-Egg Chocolate Muffins, page 139

Props courtesy of: Canhome Global

Gluten-Free Honey Muffins

*Mild spices and sweet honey flavours. Add dried cherries or
a brown sugar-cinnamon topping for attractive variations.*

White (or brown) rice flour	2 1/2 cups	625 mL
Gluten-free baking powder	1 tbsp.	15 mL
(see Tip, page 147)		
Salt	1/2 tsp.	2 mL
Ground cinnamon	1/2 tsp.	2 mL
Ground nutmeg	1/4 tsp.	1 mL
Milk	1 cup	250 mL
Vanilla yogurt	1/3 cup	75 mL
Liquid honey	1/4 cup	60 mL
Butter (or hard margarine), softened	1/2 cup	125 mL
Granulated sugar	1/2 cup	125 mL
Large eggs	2	2

Combine first 5 ingredients in medium bowl. Set aside.

Combine next 3 ingredients in small bowl.

Cream butter and sugar in large bowl. Add eggs 1 at a time, beating
well after each addition. Add flour mixture in 3 parts, alternating with
milk mixture in 2 parts, stirring after each addition until just combined.
Fill 12 greased muffin cups 3/4 full. Bake in 375°F (190°C) oven for
18 to 20 minutes until wooden pick inserted in centre of muffin comes
out clean. Let stand in pan for 5 minutes before removing to wire rack
to cool. Makes 12 muffins.

*1 muffin: 289 Calories; 9.8 g Total Fat (2.9 g Mono, 0.6 g Poly, 5.7 g Sat); 59 mg Cholesterol;
47 g Carbohydrate; 1 g Fibre; 4 g Protein; 300 mg Sodium*

GLUTEN-FREE CHERRY HONEY MUFFINS: Add 1/3 cup (75 mL) dried
cherries with last addition of milk mixture.

GLUTEN-FREE CINNAMON HONEY MUFFINS: Combine 2 tbsp. (30 mL)
packed brown sugar and 1/4 tsp. (1 mL) ground cinnamon in small cup.
Sprinkle on batter before baking.

Wheat-Free Date Muffins

With a flavour reminiscent of date squares,
these satisfying muffins are a meal in themselves.

Pitted dates, chopped	1 1/2 cups	375 mL
Water	1 cup	250 mL
Brown sugar, packed	2/3 cup	150 mL
Butter (or hard margarine)	1/2 cup	125 mL
White (or brown) rice flour	1 1/2 cups	375 mL
Soy flour	1 cup	250 mL
Quick-cooking rolled oats	2/3 cup	150 mL
Gluten-free baking powder (see Tip, below)	1 tbsp.	15 mL
Baking soda	1/2 tsp.	2 mL
Salt	1/4 tsp.	1 mL
Large egg, fork-beaten	1	1
Orange juice	1 cup	250 mL
Pecan pieces, toasted (see Tip, page 95) and chopped	1 cup	250 mL

Measure first 4 ingredients into small saucepan. Heat and stir on medium until butter is melted. Bring to a boil. Boil, uncovered, for 1 minute. Transfer to heatproof medium bowl. Cool to room temperature.

Measure next 6 ingredients into large bowl. Stir. Make a well in centre.

Add remaining 3 ingredients to date mixture. Stir. Add to well. Stir until just moistened. Fill 12 greased muffin cups full. Bake in 375°F (190°C) oven for 20 to 25 minutes until wooden pick inserted in centre of muffin comes out clean. Let stand in pan for 5 minutes before removing to wire rack to cool. Makes 12 muffins.

1 muffin: 396 Calories; 17.3 g Total Fat (7.1 g Mono, 3.1 g Poly, 6.1 g Sat); 40 mg Cholesterol; 58 g Carbohydrate; 4 g Fibre; 7 g Protein; 291 mg Sodium

 tip You can buy gluten-free baking powder or you can make your own. To make 1 tbsp. (15 mL) gluten-free baking powder, combine 2 tsp. (10 mL) cream of tartar and 1 tsp. (5 mL) baking soda. Use only the amount needed in the recipe. Store remaining amount in airtight container.

Apple Streusel Muffins

A dense, compact muffin—wheat free, milk free, no sugar added.

White rice flour	1 1/2 cups	375 mL
Oat flour (see Note)	1 cup	250 mL
Low-calorie sweetener (Splenda)	1/2 cup	125 mL
Baking powder	2 tsp.	10 mL
Baking soda	1/2 tsp.	2 mL
Salt	1/2 tsp.	2 mL
Ground cinnamon	1/2 tsp.	2 mL
Ground nutmeg	1/4 tsp.	1 mL
Large eggs	2	2
Unsweetened applesauce	1 cup	250 mL
Cooking oil	1/4 cup	60 mL
Finely chopped peeled cooking apple (such as McIntosh)	1/2 cup	125 mL
Chopped walnuts (or pecans)	1/2 cup	125 mL
TOPPING		
Finely chopped walnuts	1/4 cup	60 mL
Oat flour (see Note)	2 tbsp.	30 mL
Low-calorie sweetener (Splenda)	1 tsp.	5 mL
Ground cinnamon	1/4 tsp.	1 mL

Measure first 8 ingredients into large bowl. Stir. Make a well in centre.

Combine next 3 ingredients in medium bowl. Add to well.

Add apple and walnuts. Stir until just moistened. Fill 12 greased muffin cups 3/4 full.

Topping: Combine all 4 ingredients in small bowl. Sprinkle on batter. Bake in 375°F (190°C) oven for 18 to 20 minutes until wooden pick inserted in centre of muffin comes out clean. Let stand in pan for 5 minutes before removing to wire rack to cool. Makes 12 muffins.

1 muffin: 255 Calories; 11.8 g Total Fat (4.7 g Mono, 5.1 g Poly, 1.2 g Sat); 36 mg Cholesterol; 31 g Carbohydrate; 5 g Fibre; 7 g Protein; 225 mg Sodium

Note: To make 1 cup (250 mL) plus 2 tbsp. (30 mL) oat flour, process 1 1/4 cups (300 mL) quick-cooking rolled oats in blender or food processor until finely ground.

"Free" Muffins

Dairy-free, egg-free, gluten-free and delicious! The rice flour adds a grainy texture to these flavourful muffins.

White (or brown) rice flour	1 1/2 cups	375 mL
Soy flour	1/2 cup	125 mL
Gluten-free baking powder (see Tip, page 147)	2 tsp.	10 mL
Ground cinnamon	1 tsp.	5 mL
Baking soda	1/2 tsp.	2 mL
Ground allspice	1/4 tsp.	1 mL
Salt	1/4 tsp.	1 mL
Ground flaxseed (see Tip, page 51)	1 tbsp.	15 mL
Water	3 tbsp.	50 mL
Unsweetened applesauce	1 cup	250 mL
Brown sugar, packed	1/2 cup	125 mL
Cooking oil	1/4 cup	60 mL
Vanilla extract	1 tsp.	5 mL
Medium cooking apples (such as McIntosh), peeled and diced	2	2
Chopped pecans	1/2 cup	125 mL
TOPPING		
Chopped pecans	1/4 cup	60 mL
Brown sugar, packed	3 tbsp.	50 mL
Soy flour	1 tbsp.	15 mL
Cooking oil	1 tbsp.	15 mL

Measure first 7 ingredients into large bowl. Stir. Make a well in centre.

Process ground flaxseed and water in blender for about 1 minute until smooth. Add next 4 ingredients. Process until smooth. Add to well. Add apple and pecans. Stir until just moistened. Fill 12 greased muffin cups 3/4 full.

Topping: Combine all 4 ingredients in small bowl. Sprinkle on batter. Bake in 375°F (190°C) oven for about 20 minutes until wooden pick inserted in centre of muffin comes out clean. Let stand in pan for 5 minutes before removing to wire rack to cool. Makes 12 muffins.

1 muffin: 277 Calories; 12.8 g Total Fat (7.2 g Mono, 3.9 g Poly, 1.1 g Sat); 0 mg Cholesterol; 39 g Carbohydrate; 2 g Fibre; 4 g Protein; 172 mg Sodium

Pictured on page 144.

Measurement Tables

Throughout this book measurements are given in Conventional and Metric measure. To compensate for differences between the two measurements due to rounding, a full metric measure is not always used. The cup used is the standard 8 fluid ounce. Temperature is given in degrees Fahrenheit and Celsius. Baking pan measurements are in inches and centimetres as well as quarts and litres. An exact metric conversion is given below as well as the working equivalent (Metric Standard Measure).

Spoons

Conventional Measure	Metric Exact Conversion Millilitre (mL)	Metric Standard Measure Millilitre (mL)
1/8 teaspoon (tsp.)	0.6 mL	0.5 mL
1/4 teaspoon (tsp.)	1.2 mL	1 mL
1/2 teaspoon (tsp.)	2.4 mL	2 mL
1 teaspoon (tsp.)	4.7 mL	5 mL
2 teaspoons (tsp.)	9.4 mL	10 mL
1 tablespoon (tbsp.)	14.2 mL	15 mL

Cups

Conventional Measure	Metric Exact Conversion Millilitre (mL)	Metric Standard Measure Millilitre (mL)
1/4 cup (4 tbsp.)	56.8 mL	60 mL
1/3 cup (5 1/3 tbsp.)	75.6 mL	75 mL
1/2 cup (8 tbsp.)	113.7 mL	125 mL
2/3 cup (10 2/3 tbsp.)	151.2 mL	150 mL
3/4 cup (12 tbsp.)	170.5 mL	175 mL
1 cup (16 tbsp.)	227.3 mL	250 mL
4 1/2 cups	1022.9 mL	1000 mL (1 L)

Oven Temperatures

Fahrenheit (°F)	Celsius (°C)
175°	80°
200°	95°
225°	110°
250°	120°
275°	140°
300°	150°
325°	160°
350°	175°
375°	190°
400°	205°
425°	220°
450°	230°
475°	240°
500°	260°

Dry Measurements

Conventional Measure Ounces (oz.)	Metric Exact Conversion Grams (g)	Metric Standard Measure Grams (g)
1 oz.	28.3 g	28 g
2 oz.	56.7 g	57 g
3 oz.	85.0 g	85 g
4 oz.	113.4 g	125 g
5 oz.	141.7 g	140 g
6 oz.	170.1 g	170 g
7 oz.	198.4 g	200 g
8 oz.	226.8 g	250 g
16 oz.	453.6 g	500 g
32 oz.	907.2 g	1000 g (1 kg)

Pans

Conventional Inches	Metric Centimetres
8x8 inch	20x20 cm
9x9 inch	22x22 cm
9x13 inch	22x33 cm
10x15 inch	25x38 cm
11x17 inch	28x43 cm
8x2 inch round	20x5 cm
9x2 inch round	22x5 cm
10x4 1/2 inch tube	25x11 cm
8x4x3 inch loaf	20x10x7.5 cm
9x5x3 inch loaf	22x12.5x7.5 cm

Casseroles

CANADA & BRITAIN		UNITED STATES	
Standard Size Casserole	Exact Metric Measure	Standard Size Casserole	Exact Metric Measure
1 qt. (5 cups)	1.13 L	1 qt. (4 cups)	900 mL
1 1/2 qts. (7 1/2 cups)	1.69 L	1 1/2 qts. (6 cups)	1.35 L
2 qts. (10 cups)	2.25 L	2 qts. (8 cups)	1.8 L
2 1/2 qts. (12 1/2 cups)	2.81 L	2 1/2 qts. (10 cups)	2.25 L
3 qts. (15 cups)	3.38 L	3 qts. (12 cups)	2.7 L
4 qts. (20 cups)	4.5 L	4 qts. (16 cups)	3.6 L
5 qts. (25 cups)	5.63 L	5 qts. (20 cups)	4.5 L

Recipe Index

152

153

155

156

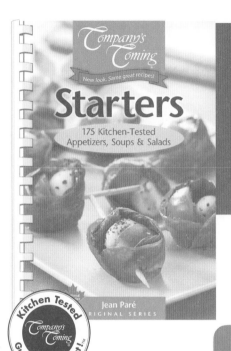

Starters

Try it

a sample recipe from *Starters*

Snackin' Potato Skins

Starters, Page 79

Medium baking potatoes, baked and cooled	5	5
Hard margarine (or butter), melted	1/4 cup	60 mL
Seasoned salt, sprinkle		

Cut potatoes in half lengthwise. Cut each half lengthwise. Now cut all 20 strips in half crosswise making 40 pieces. Scoop away most of the potato leaving a thin layer on each skin.

Brush both sides with margarine. Sprinkle with seasoned salt. Place, skin side up, on ungreased baking sheet. Bake in 400°F (205°C) oven for 10 to 15 minutes until crisp. Makes 40 pieces.

1 coated potato skin: 24 Calories; 1.1 g Total Fat; 15 mg Sodium; trace Protein; 3 g Carbohydrate; trace Dietary Fibre

Variation #1: Omit seasoned salt. Sprinkle with 1/2 envelope of taco seasoning. Bake as above. Serve with Guacamole.

Variation #2: Omit margarine and seasoned salt. Place potato wedges, skin side down, on ungreased baking sheet. Sprinkle with 1 cup (250 mL) grated Cheddar cheese. Add either 1/3 cup (75 mL) cooked and crumbled bacon or 1/3 cup (75 mL) chopped green onion, or a combination of both. Bake as above.

Celebrating the
Harvest
RECIPES FOR FALL & WINTER GATHERINGS

Whether from the garden, farmers' market or supermarket, harvest ingredients display the bounty and beauty of nature. Entertain a crowd in style, or feed your family comfort food they'll not soon forget—with new delicious recipes that celebrate harvest ingredients. What a lovely way to get through the long fall and winter!

SPECIAL OCCASION SERIES

If you like what we've done with **cooking,** you'll **love** what we do with **crafts!**